MW01705153

BMSC's Specialty Certification Learning Series

Study Guide for

HCS-D Certification Examinations

Updated per 2013 Prospective Payment System (M1024) instructions, effective January 1, 2013.

By **Sharon Molinari, RN, HCS-D, HCS-O**

Board of
Medical Specialty
Coding & Compliance

Published by:

The Board of Medical Specialty Coding & Compliance
Two Washingtonian Center
9737 Washingtonian Blvd., Ste. 200
Gaithersburg, MD 20878-7364
www.medicalspecialtycoding.com

ISBN: 978-1-935477-26-6

H5372

Table of Contents

Introduction

Congratulations on your decision to advance in your coding career by earning the Home Care Coding Specialist – Diagnosis (HCS-D) certification or recertification!

This credential is evidence of your coding proficiency and can provide additional professional and personal recognition and reward. Certified coders are in high demand for their ability to ensure compliance and appropriate reimbursement.

With the ongoing changes in home health coding, staying compliant and on top of issues is a challenge.

The HCS-D examinations assess your proficiency in home care coding by testing your knowledge of the Official Coding Guidelines, conventions and regulatory issues, as well as medical terminology, and your ability to apply them. Developed for home care coders by a team of home care coding experts, these examinations are updated annually and are reviewed for accuracy and relevance on a regular basis.

Use this guide in conjunction with the study outlines, located at the back of this book, to prepare for the HCS-D certification and recertification examinations.

Terminology and Concepts

A working knowledge of medical terminology is necessary to select the appropriate diagnosis codes which "paint the picture" of a patient's health status and how it supports the need for home care services. Coders must translate the descriptions of diseases, injuries, conditions and procedures into a number. This process is complex.

The ability to code accurately is imperative for compliance with the official coding guidelines and regulations, and to obtain appropriate reimbursement for the agency. Correct coding relies upon experience, knowledge of the coding guidelines and conventions, and understanding of medical language such as diseases, terms and abbreviations. It is necessary for every coder to have available current reference tools such as a coding manual, Chapter 3 and Appendix D of the OASIS-C Guidance Manual, a medical dictionary and a drug book or the ability to access this information online.

As you proceed through this study guide, be sure to have these tools available and, if you're not sure of a term, guideline or concept, take the time to familiarize yourself with it. Though you will not be tested on medical terminology, you are expected to know it, as it is incorporated into the scenarios on the examinations.

ICD-9-CM Official Coding Guidelines and Conventions

The ICD-9-CM Official Guidelines for Coding and Reporting and the Conventions are specific guidelines and general rules that are applicable to all health care settings, unless otherwise indicated.

The official coding guidelines are based on the coding and sequencing instructions in Volumes 1, 2 and 3 of the ICD-9-CM, but provide additional instruction. Adherence to these guidelines when assigning diagnosis and procedure codes is required under the Health Insurance Portability and Accountability Act (HIPAA). The HIPAA Administrative Simplification Rule, effective Oct. 16, 2003, instructs that every provider and every payor must follow the same coding guidelines and that all claims must be in compliance with the coding rules.

These guidelines have been developed to assist both the health care provider and the coder in identifying those diagnoses and procedures that are to be reported. The importance of consistent, complete documentation in the medical record cannot be overemphasized! Without such documentation, accurate coding cannot be achieved. The entire medical record should be reviewed to determine the specific reason for the encounter, the conditions treated and pertinent history.

Periodic revisions are made to the official coding guidelines. The most recent revisions, effective 10/01/11, can be found at: *www.cdc.gov/nchs/data/icd9/9cmguidelines2011.pdf.*

Revisions are made annually to Volumes 1, 2, and 3 of the ICD-9-CM coding manual. The changes, which vary from year to year, take effect on Oct. 1 and include:

- New ICD-9-CM codes
- Deletion of old ICD-9-CM codes
- Addition of 4th and 5th digits for more specificity
- Revisions to descriptors
- The coding revisions that took effect Oct. 1, 2011 can be found at: *www.cdc.gov/nchs/icd/icd9cm_addenda_guidelines.htm#addenda.*

However, due to the planned implementation of ICD-10-CM on Oct. 1, 2014, there was a code freeze in 2012, and it is anticipated that there will be only limited updates to both code sets in 2013 for new technologies and diseases and to ICD-10 in 2014. Beginning October 1, 2015, there will be regular updates to ICD-10.

Publishers of the ICD-9-CM volumes use a variety of symbols or formatting conventions to identify changes in their manual. It is imperative that you always use a ***current*** coding manual and that you know your manual well.

Coding Conventions

The conventions are the general rules for use of the classification independent of the guidelines. They include abbreviations, punctuation, symbols, typefaces, formatting methods and rules.

The two sources of ICD-9-CM coding conventions are the ICD-9-CM Official Guidelines for Coding and Reporting and the ICD-9-CM publisher-specific formatting conventions. The coding conventions are incorporated within the Alphabetic Index and the Tabular List of the ICD-9-CM coding manual as instructional notes.

Tip! *Read these notes to find important instructions. This concept is tested on the HCS-D exam.*

The coding conventions are as follows:

Format

The ICD-9-CM uses an indented format for ease of reference.

Abbreviations

NEC, not elsewhere classifiable, means "other specified" and is found in both the Alphabetic Index and Tabular List when the ICD-9-CM system does not provide a more specific code for a condition. NEC means you have the information, but there is no specific code allocated. For example, see Infection, Bacillus NEC.

NOS, not otherwise specified, is the equivalent of "unspecified" and is only used when information in the medical record is insufficient to assign a more specific code. NOS is noted in the Tabular List. For example, see 490 Bronchitis NOS.

Tip! *Consider whether you have more specific information in the scenario before selecting an NOS code.*

Punctuation

[ ] Brackets:

- Enclose synonyms, alternative wording or explanatory phrases in the Tabular List
    - e.g., Pneumonia due to Hemophilus influenzae [H. influenzae]
- Include the numbers acceptable for the 5th digit
    - e.g., 715.0 Osteoarthrosis, generalized
      [0, 4, 9]
      The numbers within the brackets are the only options that may be selected for the 5th digit.

[ ] Slanted Brackets are used in the Alphabetic Index to identify *manifestation codes* and to indicate *mandatory multiple coding*. Both codes must be assigned to describe the condition and are sequenced in the order listed.

- e.g., 266.9 *[357.4]* Polyneuropathy in Vitamin B deficiency

( ) Parentheses are used in both the Alphabetic Index and the Tabular List to enclose supplementary words that may be present or absent in the statement of a disease or procedure without affecting the code assignment. The terms within the parentheses are referred to as *nonessential modifiers*.

- e.g., Bronchiolitis in the Alphabetic Index
    - Bronchiolitis (acute) (infectious) (subacute) 466.19
- e.g., 491.2x in the Tabular List
    - Obstructive chronic bronchitis
      Bronchitis:
      emphysematous
      obstructive (chronic) (diffuse)

Note: *Nonessential modifiers are in parentheses after the term they modify. These modifiers do not affect the code selection. Essential modifiers are indented under the main term in the Alphabetic Index. They do affect the code selection and must be specified in the physician's diagnostic statement (e.g., Lobar pneumonia).*

: Colons are used in the Tabular List after an incomplete term that needs one or more of the modifiers following the colon to make it assignable to a given category.

- e.g., 250.7 Diabetes with peripheral circulatory disorders
  Use additional code to identify manifestation as:
  diabetic:
  gangrene (785.4)
  peripheral angiopathy (443.81)

Includes and Excludes Notes and Inclusion Terms

"Includes" and "Excludes" notes and "inclusion terms" are found in Volume 1 of the Tabular List, and will help you select the correct code.

INCLUDES: This note appears immediately under a three-digit code title to further define or give examples of the content of a category. Look at Category 402, Hypertensive heart disease.

EXCLUDES: This note under a code indicates that the terms excluded from the code are to be coded elsewhere.

Tip! *Pay close attention to exclusions, because this means you are not in the right place! Look at Category 401, Essential hypertension.*

Inclusion Terms: These terms may be included under certain four and five-digit codes and are the conditions for which the code is to be used. The terms may be synonyms of the code title, or, in the case of "other specified" codes, the terms are a list of the various conditions assigned to that code. The inclusion terms are not necessarily exhaustive. Look at codes 428.0 and 722.10. Additional terms found only in the Alphabetic Index may also be assigned to a code. For example, under the main term "Gait" in the Alphabetic Index, the subterm "scissor 781.2" is included. In the Tabular List, the inclusion terms under code 781.2 do not include "scissor." However, since the coder is directed in the Index to 781.2 for a "scissor" gait, that is the correct code.

Etiology/Manifestation Convention

Certain conditions have both an underlying etiology and multiple body system manifestations due to the underlying etiology. For such conditions, the ICD-9-CM has a coding convention that requires the underlying condition be sequenced first, followed by the manifestation. Wherever such a combination exists, there is a "use additional code" note at the etiology code, and a "code first" note at the manifestation code. These instructional notes indicate the proper sequencing of the codes – the etiology immediately followed by the manifestation.

In most cases, titles of manifestation codes will include the phrase "in diseases classified elsewhere." Codes with this title are a component of the etiology/manifestation convention. The code title indicates that it is a manifestation code.

There are manifestation codes that do not have "in diseases classified elsewhere" in the title. For such codes, a "code first" note will still be present and the same rules for sequencing apply.

In addition to the notes in the Tabular List, these conditions also have a specific entry structure in the Alphabetic Index. In the Index, both conditions are listed together, with the etiology code first followed by the manifestation code in italics and slanted brackets. The etiology is always sequenced first and the manifestation code is sequenced second. This does not mean that they have to be the primary diagnosis and the first secondary diagnosis. Sequencing will depend on the seriousness of the condition related to the care plan. However, they must be sequenced together: etiology first, immediately followed by the manifestation.

The most common etiology/manifestation combinations are for Diabetes mellitus, Category 250, and Secondary diabetes mellitus, Category 249. For each 249 and 250 code with manifestations, there is a "use additional code" note for that particular diabetic manifestation. The 249 and 250 diabetes codes are sequenced first, followed by the manifestation codes.

"Code first" and "use additional code" notes are also used as sequencing rules in the classification for certain codes that are not part of an etiology/manifestation combination. **"Code first"** indicates a manifestation code or signals the need to code an underlying condition first. **"Use additional code"** alerts the coder that an additional code should be used, if the information is available, to provide a more complete picture of that diagnosis.

Case-mix manifestations are designated with a capital 'M' in the current CMS (Centers for Medicare and Medicaid Services) case-mix list.

Tip! *Understanding the coding guidelines for manifestations is imperative in order to earn the HCS-D certification.*

"And"

"And" can mean either "and" or "or" when it appears in the title. (e.g., Abscess of lung and mediastinum)

"With"

"With" in the Index is sequenced immediately following the main term, not in alphabetical order (e.g., Asthma with COPD).

"See" and "See Also"

"See" following a main term in the Index indicates that another term should be referenced. It is necessary to go to the main term referenced with the "see" note to locate the correct code. (e.g., Dementia – Alzheimer's – *see* Alzheimer's, dementia)

"See also" following a main term in the Index instructs that there is another main term you can reference that may provide additional useful entries. It is not necessary to follow the "see also" note when the original main term provides the necessary code. (e.g., Virus, viral [*see also* condition]).

Level of Detail in Coding

Diagnoses and procedures are to be coded to the highest number of digits available.

ICD-9-CM diagnosis codes are composed of three, four, or five digits. Codes with three digits are a category of codes that may be further subdivided by the use of 4th and/or 5th digits, which provide greater detail. The more digits, the more specific the information is. You must look for indications that there are 4th or 5th digits.

Three-digit ***categories*** are to be used only if they are not further subdivided. Where 4th-digit ***subcategories*** and/or 5th-digit ***subclassifications*** are provided, they must be assigned. A code is invalid if it has not been coded to the full number of digits required for that code. For example, Category 715, Osteoarthrosis and allied disorders, has 4th digits that describe the type (e.g., localized or primary), and 5th digits that identify the site. It would be incorrect to report a code in Category 715 without a 4th and 5th digit.

Volume 3, procedure codes, is composed of codes with either three or four digits. Codes with two digits are included in ICD-9-CM as the heading of a category of codes that may be further subdivided by the use of 3rd and/or 4th digits, which provide greater detail.

Tip! *One of the most common coding errors is leaving digits off, so make sure the codes you select have all the required digits.*

OASIS, Coding, PPS and Billing

According to the Medicare Claims Processing Manual, the codes for all diagnoses, primary and secondary, must match on the OASIS, plan of care (POC) and the UB-04 Claim Form. The Prospective Payment System (PPS) provides split percentage payments to home health agencies.

- Request for Anticipated Payment (RAP)
  - 60% of the anticipated episode rate is paid at Start of Care (SOC)
  - 50% upon Recertification
- Final or End of Episode (EOE) Claim
  - The remaining 40% is paid for SOCs and 50% for Recertifications
  - Adjustments are made – e.g., therapy threshold not met

The diagnosis codes on the RAP should always match the codes on the final billing claim.

If there is a change in diagnoses after the RAP has been submitted, it must be cancelled and re-submitted with the correct diagnoses. The POC and OASIS must also be corrected. *Remember, the diagnoses must match on all 3 forms — OASIS, POC, and billing claim.*

The Health Insurance Portability and Accountability Act (HIPAA) Code and Transaction Set requires that the billing claim be compliant with HIPAA, which mandates that only unresolved diagnoses be reported. Diagnoses in M1020a (Primary Diagnosis), M1022b-f and other pertinent diagnoses (Other Diagnoses) are entered on the billing claim. Items in M1024 Column 3 and Column 4 (Payment Diagnoses) are not reported in any field of the billing claim form. Therefore, the diagnoses in M1024 do **not** have to be compliant with HIPAA, just OASIS requirements. For this reason, a fracture code or a resolved condition may be placed in M1024 Column 3, but not in M1020, M1022, or as another diagnosis.

Note: *The 2013 PPS Final Rule for home health, effective January 1, 2013, restricts payment to only acute fracture codes, which cannot be reported as primary or other (secondary) diagnoses, when placed in M1024 across from M1020 or M1022 and paired with an appropriate V code.*

This will be discussed further under M1024 (Payment Diagnoses).

OASIS Guidance on Diagnoses

As a general rule, you will be tested on M1020a, M1022b-f and M1024. Other OASIS diagnosis items, M1010, M1012 and M1016, are not included in scenarios, but you must know the coding guidelines for these.

M1010: Inpatient Diagnosis

M1010 identifies the diagnosis(es) for which the patient *received active treatment* during an inpatient stay within the past 14 days. This period encompasses the two weeks immediately preceding the start/resumption of care and refers to the inpatient facility discharge. For the purpose of counting the 14-day period, the start/resumption of care date is day 0 and the day immediately preceding this date is day 1.

This item is intended to allow for a more comprehensive picture of the patient's condition prior to the initiation of home care.

List up to six diagnoses that were ***actively* treated** any time during an inpatient facility stay with a discharge date within the 14 days immediately preceding the start of care or resumption of care. These could be new diagnoses or exacerbations of chronic conditions and may or may not correspond with the hospital diagnoses.

"Active treatment" means receiving something more than the regularly scheduled medications and treatments necessary to maintain or treat an existing diagnosis.

If a diagnosis was not ***actively treated*** during an inpatient admission, do ***not*** list it. For example, the patient has a long-standing history of hypertension, for which the medication was continued during the hospital stay, but was treated only for pneumonia. Do ***not*** list hypertension as an inpatient diagnosis.

Do ***not*** list symptoms when the condition/disease is known.

More points to remember about M1010:

- Determine the "past 14 days" by looking at a calendar. Determine the day of the week for SOC/ROC.
- Look back to the same day 2 weeks previous. Inpatient stays with facility discharges occurring on or between these days are "the past 14 days." Specified timeframes must be strictly adhered to!
- May be a numeric code only
- No V codes or E codes allowed – list the underlying diagnosis
- No surgical codes allowed – report the underlying condition

For example, a patient had a colostomy due to malignant colon cancer and was discharged from the hospital 2 days prior to admission to home care. The diagnosis in M1010 would be malignant colon cancer – 153.9.

M1012: Inpatient Procedures

M1012 identifies medical procedures that the patient received any time during an inpatient facility stay with a discharge within the past 14 days that are *relevant* to the plan of care (i.e., a joint replacement that requires home rehabilitation services).

Up to four medical procedures ***may*** be listed in M1012. Reporting procedures in this item is now ***optional***. CMS said that the response reported will have no impact on risk adjustment, quality measure reporting or reimbursement under the Home Health Prospective Payment System. This item must be completed, though. Home health agencies may report procedures and codes, **or** "UK," **or** "NA."

The procedure codes are found in Volume 3 of the ICD-9-CM coding manual.

M1016: Diagnoses Requiring Changed Medical Regimen

M1016 identifies whether any changes have occurred to the patient's treatment regimen, health care services or medications within the past 14 days. This timeframe encompasses the two-week period immediately preceding the start/resumption of care date or the date of the agency discharge visit.

The purpose of this question is to identify the patient's history by identifying new diagnoses or diagnoses that have exacerbated over the past 2 weeks. This information helps the clinician develop an appropriate plan of care, since patients who have recent changes in treatment plans have a higher risk of becoming unstable.

The response to this item may include the same diagnoses as M1010, if the condition was treated during an inpatient stay AND caused changes in the treatment regimen within the past 14 days.

List up to six diagnoses that required a change in the patient's medications or treatments (wound care, diet, pain management, activity, therapy, etc.) within the past 14 days.

Mark "NA" if there were no medical or treatment regimen changes within the past 14 days or if changes in the medical or treatment regimen were made because a diagnosis improved — e.g., antibiotic for pneumonia discontinued or change from insulin to an oral medication.

A physician appointment by itself or a referral for home health services does ***not*** qualify as a medical or treatment regimen change.

All treatments and disciplines ordered at SOC do ***not*** count as a change, but changes during the episode ***do*** count as a change (e.g., discontinuation of therapy services).

More points to remember about M1016:

- May be a numeric code only
- No V codes or E codes allowed – list the underlying diagnosis
- No surgical codes allowed – report the underlying condition

Tip! *A change that results from the assessment visit is considered a change for M1016.*

M1020: Primary Diagnosis

The primary diagnosis is defined as the diagnosis most related to the current home health plan of care. It represents the most acute condition that requires the most intensive ***skilled*** services. The most acute condition is not necessarily the patient's most serious condition. It is the one which is the main focus of home care. For example, a patient with ESRD may be admitted for wound care to a pressure ulcer. Even though the ESRD is the patient's most acute or serious condition, the focus of care is the pressure ulcer, so that would be the primary diagnosis.

The primary diagnosis may or may not be related to the most recent hospital stay, but must relate to the services rendered by the home health agency. The primary diagnosis best reflects the care being provided for the entire episode and may best be described by a V code. Consider services, medications, treatments and procedures.

If more than one diagnosis meets the definition of primary diagnosis, either condition may be sequenced first.

If a patient is admitted for surgical aftercare, list the relevant medical diagnosis, only if it is still applicable. If it is no longer applicable (e.g., the surgery eliminated the condition or the acute phase has ended), then a V code, such as for surgical aftercare, is generally appropriate as the primary diagnosis. An example is a patient who is admitted to home care for surgical aftercare following an ORIF of a hip fracture. Coding guidelines stipulate that the acute fracture code may only be used for the initial, acute episode of care, which is why the acute fracture code is no longer appropriate once the patient has been admitted to home care. In this case, a V code for aftercare of the healing fracture would be the appropriate primary diagnosis, if both nursing and therapy are ordered. If the case is therapy-only, the appropriate V57 code would be assigned as the primary diagnosis followed by the aftercare code.

The diagnosis in M1020 is the principal diagnosis in Field 11 of the plan of care and is the first-listed diagnosis on the billing claim form. This diagnosis code, and the secondary ones, must match in all three places – the OASIS, the plan of care and the claim form.

Points to remember about M1020:

- It may be a numeric code or it may be a V code.
- It may never be an E code.

M1022: Other Diagnoses

Other diagnoses, or secondary diagnoses, are defined as all conditions that coexisted at the time the plan of care was established, **or** which developed subsequently, **or** affect the treatment or care. Include all ***pertinent*** diagnoses relevant to the care being rendered. List the diagnoses in the order that best reflects the seriousness of the patient's condition related to the care plan. Remember, this is determined by which diagnoses will require the most intensive skilled home care services during the current episode of care.

Ensure that the secondary diagnoses include ***not only*** conditions actively addressed in the patient's plan of care ***but also*** any comorbidity affecting the patient's responsiveness to treatment and rehabilitative prognosis, even if the condition is not the focus of home health treatment itself.

A comorbidity is simply a disease or condition co-existing with the primary disease. For example, the primary disease may be emphysema and the comorbidity may be hypertension.

The presence of comorbidities helps to show the complexity of the patient's condition.

Certain comorbidities should *always* be coded because they may impact or be impacted by the patient's care plan, even in the absence of documented active intervention. These include but are not limited to:

- Diabetes mellitus
- Hypertension (HTN)

- Peripheral vascular disease (PVD)
- Coronary artery disease (CAD)
- Asthma
- Emphysema
- Chronic obstructive pulmonary disease (COPD)
- Congestive heart failure (CHF) or any type of heart failure
- Chronic neurological diseases, such as Parkinson's, Alzheimer's, and multiple sclerosis
- Blindness, if it impacts the care plan
- Amputation status
- History of a neoplasm, if there is a current neoplasm

These diagnoses impact the care plan and should be listed, even if therapy is the only service provided. Diagnoses on the OASIS (M1020a and M1022b-f) ***must*** be addressed in the plan of care – assessment, monitoring, or treatment.

Other comorbidities such as anemia, GERD and low vision should also be coded, if the documentation supports their impact on the plan of care and the need for intervention. It would be upcoding, if these case-mix diagnoses were reported on the OASIS when they are not relevant to the current plan of care.

Other diagnoses that have no impact on the care plan, are historical in nature, or are not relevant to the episode of care should **not** be coded.

Documentation in the medical record ***must*** support the diagnosis codes and the services provided. It is imperative that ***all*** diagnoses be documented or verified by the physician!

Tip! *Knowing the criteria for selecting secondary diagnoses, including comorbidities, is crucial for the HCS-D exams.*

The first secondary diagnosis, which is listed in M1022b, appears first in Field 13 on the plan of care. It may be a manifestation diagnosis if a manifestation is the primary focus of care. For example, if diabetic neuropathy is the focus of care, neuropathy will be listed in M1022b and diabetes in M1020a.

Points to remember about M1022:

- There is no M1022a. The first M1022 is M1022b, because M1020 is primary and it takes the "a" slot.
- May be numeric codes, V codes or E codes
- E codes are allowed in M1022 or as other diagnoses only!

Remember these coding tips:

- A disease may be reported more than once because of multiple manifestations.
    - e.g., 250.8x, 707.1x (Diabetic ulcer)
      250.5x, 369.4 (Diabetic blindness)
- Duplicate ICD-9 codes cannot be listed on the plan of care or billing claim form.
    - e.g., Osteoarthritis bilateral knees can only be coded once.

M1024: Payment Diagnoses

M1024 is an <u>optional</u> OASIS item intended to facilitate PPS payment when a V code is reported as the primary diagnosis <u>or</u> as a secondary diagnosis in place of a case-mix diagnosis used to determine the PPS case-mix. This applies to Medicare or other payors that require a HHRG/HIPPS code for payment.

Case-mix points will be awarded only for acute fractures when placed in M1024 and paired with an appropriate V code from Table 25 – Fracture Conditions and Appropriate V codes. These are V54.1x and V54.2x. (See this table in the back of the study guide.)

To earn the points, the variables in the Case-Mix Adjustment Variables and Scores (also in the back of the study guide) must be met. Fracture codes add points to the clinical domain as Ortho 1 or Ortho 2 diagnoses.

An Ortho 1 diagnosis will only earn case-mix points if the patient has a pressure ulcer and is in an early episode (first or second adjacent episode of care) with 0-13 therapy visits OR is in an early episode and is receiving IV or parenteral therapy at home (M1030 = 1 or 2). A patient with an Ortho 2 diagnosis must be receiving an IV/infusion or parenteral therapy (M1030 = 1 or 2) and be in an early episode of care with 0-14+ therapy visits in order to earn the points.

Resolved case-mix diagnoses related to the plan of care that may be significant in describing the patient ***may*** be listed in M1024 for possible risk adjustment. However, these resolved conditions will receive risk adjustment, if applicable, if they are listed in M1010 or M1016. If placed in M1024, these diagnoses will ***not*** be awarded case-mix points.

Case-mix diagnoses placed in M1024 must be determined in accordance with OASIS requirements in effect before Oct. 1, 2003 – no V codes, E codes or surgical codes allowed. Instead, code the relevant medical diagnosis.

The 2013 Final Rule permits equivalent scoring of the HHRG when the diagnosis groups that yield more points as primary than secondary – Diabetes, Skin 1 and Neuro 1 – are listed ***immediately following*** the V code in M1020, without using the payment slot (M1024).

The home health Grouper also permits more codes to act "as if" they are primary when ***immediately preceded*** by a designated V code in M1020. (See this table at the back of the study guide.)

Tip! *Resolved case-mix diagnoses that do not earn points will not be placed in M1024 on the HCS-D exams.*

M1024 examples:

1. A patient had surgery for a herniated disc in the thoracic region. The V code in M1020 is V58.78, Aftercare following surgery of the musculoskeletal system (conditions classifiable to 710-739). The underlying diagnosis to that V code is 722.11, displacement of thoracic intervertebral disc, which is a case-mix diagnosis. Because there has been surgery, the herniated disc no longer exists, so it may ***not*** be coded in M1022. The codes in M1022 may be other conditions, like paresthesia, abnormality of gait, etc. You ***may*** place the resolved case-mix diagnosis and code in M1024 Column 3 for possible risk adjustment. However, risk adjustment will be gained for placement of this diagnosis in M1010 or M1016. Case-mix points will not be earned for this resolved condition. M1024 Column 4 will be blank. 722.11 will not be listed in M1022b, since it was resolved with the surgery.
2. A patient had a foot amputation due to diabetic PVD. The focus of care is aftercare following surgery for the amputation. The V

code in M1020 will be V58.73, Aftercare following surgery of the circulatory system. Diabetic PVD, 443.81, is classifiable to the stated codes, 390-459. Since PVD is stated as "diabetic PVD," it is a manifestation of diabetes, a case-mix diagnosis. Therefore, the principles for manifestation coding apply. Since the V code reported in M1020 replaces a case-mix diagnosis in one of the HH PPS diagnosis groups that earn more points as primary than secondary, diabetes will be placed in M1022b, immediately following the V code, and PVD will be placed in M1022c. If sequenced this way, the primary case mix points will be awarded for diabetes. This etiology and manifestation pairing should ***not*** be placed in M1024.

3. A patient is admitted for aftercare following an ORIF for a fracture of the hip, which resulted from a fall at home. The patient also has diabetes. The correct aftercare code is V54.13, which is an appropriate V code for the acute hip fracture, 820.8, in Table 25 and is listed as the primary diagnosis (M1020). The hip fracture, 820.8, will be placed in M1024 for potential case-mix points. In order to earn points, the variables listed in the Case-Mix Adjustment Variables and Scores must be met. This diagnosis is not listed in M1022, since fractures may NEVER be coded in M1020, M1022 or as an other diagnosis. It is not necessary to code abnormality of gait, which is considered to be integral to lower extremity fractures. Diabetes is a comorbidity that should always be coded, so that is listed in M1022b.

CMS requires that the resolved payment diagnosis(es) in M1024 must appear on the plan of care.

Unless your software allows the resolved case-mix diagnosis(es) to be placed at the bottom of the other pertinent diagnoses in Field 13 without being listed on the final claim or your agency lists them elsewhere on the plan of care, it is suggested that they be noted in Field 21. For example, a notation such as *"The case-mix diagnosis in M1024 = 812.20, Fracture of unspecified part of humerus"* may be made.

Remember:

- The PPS grouper will award case-mix points ONLY when:
    1. A V code is reported in M1020 or M1022 AND

2. The V code is paired with a fracture code from the PPS pairing list (Table 25).

- Resolved case-mix diagnoses related to the plan of care that ***may*** be significant in describing the patient may be reported in M1024. However, points will <u>not</u> be awarded for these diagnoses.
- When a code from the Diabetes, Skin 1 or Neuro 1 case-mix diagnosis group is listed immediately after the appropriate V code in the primary diagnosis slot (M1020), primary case-mix points will be awarded.

Tip! *M1024 is for payment purposes only. Payment is restricted to acute fracture codes when paired with an appropriate V code in Table 25.*

M1024 Exercises:

What are the underlying diagnoses and would you put them in M1024? How about M1022?

1. **V53.6, Fitting and adjustment of a urinary catheter**
   If attention to a Foley catheter is the focus of home care, you would choose V53.6 as the primary diagnosis. If the reason for the catheter is urinary incontinence or retention, you would **not** put either of those diagnoses in M1024 because they are ***not*** resolved nor are they case-mix diagnoses. The urinary incontinence or retention still exists, so it would be placed in M1022.
2. **V58.78, Aftercare following surgery of musculoskeletal system (due to cervical spondylosis)**
   If the surgery resolved the cervical spondylosis, it ***may*** be coded in M1024 Column 3, because it is a case-mix diagnosis. However, no case-mix points would be earned. Since surgery eliminated the problem, it would ***not*** be placed in M1022.
3. **V58.42, Aftercare following surgery for removal of a brain neoplasm**
   A brain neoplasm is a Neuro 1 case-mix diagnosis that earns more points as primary than secondary. If the patient is receiving treatment (e.g., radiation or chemotherapy), or if it is not known whether further treatment will be required, the

neoplasm is considered to be active and should be listed in M1022b immediately after the V code. If so, the primary case-mix points will be awarded.

4. **V54.12, Aftercare for healing fracture of lower arm (following traumatic fracture of the shaft of the radius and ulna)**
   813.23, Closed fracture of the radius with ulna, is a case-mix diagnosis that is paired with an appropriate V code from Table 25. Therefore, it should be placed in M1024 for potential case-mix points. Since it is a violation of the coding and HIPAA guidelines to code a fracture as an active diagnosis, it may ***not*** be listed in M1022.
5. **V54.81, Aftercare following joint replacement (due to a traumatic shoulder fracture)**
   812.00, Fracture upper end of humerus, is a case-mix diagnosis that ***may*** be placed in M1024. However, it will not earn case-mix points, since V54.81 is not listed in Table 25 as an appropriate V code pairing. The fracture code may ***not*** be placed in M1022.

Sequencing Hints

The first step in appropriate sequencing is a great assessment! Determining the relevant diagnoses and procedures is the next step to accurate coding.

Choose the diagnosis that is the chief reason for providing ***skilled*** services as the primary diagnosis, which is not necessarily the same as the inpatient primary diagnosis.

When determining the diagnoses, ask yourself:

- What is the focus of care – the most serious condition related to the care plan?
- What other diagnoses will impact the care or need interventions?
- Are there any other diagnoses that may impact the care, or be impacted by it, even if there are no active interventions?

The secret to sequencing is prioritizing the care. All pertinent diagnoses must be listed on the plan of care in the order of their ***seriousness*** related to the care plan to justify the services being rendered.

Rate the *degree of symptom control* for each numeric diagnosis from **<u>0-4</u>**, according to the scale on the OASIS included with the instructions for diagnosis coding. Do ***not*** assign symptom control ratings for V or E codes.

Note: *Only the assessing clinician can determine the primary and secondary diagnoses and assign the symptom control rating. A coder may assign the codes.*

Though the rating for symptom control of each diagnosis may assist in sequencing the diagnoses, OASIS-C instructions state that this rating should <u>not</u> be used to determine the sequencing of the diagnoses. These are separate items and sequencing may not coincide. Sequencing of diagnoses should reflect the seriousness of each condition related to the care plan and support the disciplines and services provided.

For example:

- When the focus of care is the manifestation and the etiology is controlled (e.g., diabetic ulcer), the etiology will be listed first, according to the guidelines for mandatory multiple coding, even though the symptom control rating for the ulcer would be higher than the diabetes.
- Unless a V code must be primary (such as surgical aftercare that is the focus of care or therapy only) or aftercare is relevant to the plan of care but is not the primary focus, place the code at the bottom of the diagnosis list for better risk adjustment on outcomes and to provide space on the OASIS for the pertinent comorbidities, many of which are case-mix.

  Note: *Coding guidelines state that the sequencing of multiple aftercare codes is discretionary. Therefore, codes such as attention to surgical dressing, V58.31, or attention to an ostomy, unless it is one of the 3 V codes that are case-mix – V55.0 (Tracheostomy), V55.5 (Cystostomy), or V55.6 (Urostomy) – may be sequenced after the numeric codes.*

ICD-9-CM sequencing requirements must be followed, if mandatory multiple coding is indicated for any diagnosis. The etiology or underlying condition must be coded first, immediately followed by the manifestation.

The purpose of the symptom control ratings is for risk adjustment on patient outcomes.

Risk adjustment attempts to adjust for differences in client population that may bias the outcomes. It maximizes the ability to make fair comparisons across providers and is essential when comparing quality of care when home health agencies provided services to populations with different characteristics. For example, if the average age of your patients is 5 years older than another agency, your outcomes will most likely be less favorable without risk adjustment.

Pay attention to hints in the medical record and keep in mind these sequencing tips:

- "Due to" indicates a cause of a condition: Code the cause first.
  - e.g., CHF due to HTN
    - HTN
    - CHF
- Exceptions:
  - When the condition misrepresents the focus of care
    - e.g., Monthly foley change for incontinence due to multiple sclerosis (MS)
      Fitting and adjustment of urinary catheter, V53.6
      Urinary incontinence, 788.30
      Multiple sclerosis, 340
  - When treatment/management is only for a secondary condition
    - e.g., Focus of treatment is anemia due to breast cancer
      Anemia in neoplastic disease, 285.22
      Malignant neoplasm of breast, 174.9
- "With" indicates a condition is secondary or that one condition is linked to another.
  - e.g., Acute cystitis with hematuria
    - Acute cystitis, 595.0
    - Hematuria, 599.70
  - e.g., Diabetes with ESRD
    - Diabetes with renal manifestations, 250.40
    - ESRD, 585.6

- Exception: when the coding guidelines state specific instructions regarding a causal relationship
  - e.g., Category 402 – CHF with HTN is not linked, unless the documentation states "due to hypertension" or "hypertensive heart disease."

Case-Mix

Payment for all Medicare providers paid on a prospective payment system is based on a case-mix. The *OASIS data set* is used to collect the data necessary for the "case-mix adjustment."

The data elements describe three dimensions – Clinical Severity, Functional Status, and Service Utilization – which determine the resources needed to care for the patient and the case-mix group or HHRG.

The HHRG (Home Health Resource Group), also known as the case-mix group, CFS score, or grouper, is derived from certain OASIS data elements in the *three dimensions*, and determines the patient's resource use.

- Clinical Severity (3 levels – C1-C3)
- Functional Status (3 levels – F1-F3)
- Service Utilization (5 levels – S1-S5)

There are 153 case-mix weights that determine the episode payment rate, which is case-mix adjusted.

Case-Mix Diagnoses

CMS analyzed home care claims data and developed a list of diagnoses that contribute to the case-mix.

A case-mix diagnosis is a diagnosis that contributes to the Medicare Home Health PPS case-mix group assignment. Points are attached to certain diagnoses in the clinical dimension that are determined to be associated with higher resource use.

There is a complex system for case-mix point values. A single diagnosis code is worth different point values depending on whether it is primary or secondary, used in combination with other diagnoses or specific OASIS data elements, the episode timing ("early" or "later" episode), and the number of therapy visits. For example, case-mix points will be earned if a patient's primary or secondary diagnosis is malignant neoplasm of the brain (Neuro 1) and if M1810 or M1820 (dressing upper or lower body) = 1, 2, or 4. The points will vary (either 2 or 4), depending on the episode and number of therapy visits made. In addition, 3, 5, or 8 case-mix points will be gained if it is the primary diagnosis, depending on the episode and the number of therapy visits.

A test-taker must understand how to use case-mix codes accurately. Knowledge of the variables and number of case-mix points will <u>not</u> be tested. Most coding manuals have a symbol that identifies the case-mix diagnoses.

See the Case-Mix Adjustment Variables and Scores Table at the back of this guide.

Manifestations and Mandatory Multiple Coding

Manifestations are characteristics, signs or symptoms of an illness. When one disease or condition causes another disease or condition, the one that caused it is the etiology, and the resulting second condition is the manifestation.

According to the coding guidelines, manifestation codes must be preceded by the code for the underlying condition or etiology. For example, the code for gangrene, which is a manifestation of diabetes, would be listed immediately after the diabetes code – 250.7x, 785.4.

This is called *mandatory sequencing* or *mandatory multiple coding.* When a manifestation is the primary focus of care, it is listed in M1022b, immediately following the etiology, which must be the primary diagnosis (M1020).

A manifestation may never be the primary diagnosis or coded by itself. *The etiology and the manifestation must be coded together.* When such a combination exists, there is a "use additional code" note at the etiology code and a "code first underlying disease" note at the manifestation code.

Manifestation coding conventions are as follows:

- Manifestation codes are in slanted brackets *[ ]* in the Alphabetic Index following the etiology code.
    - e.g., Cryptococcal meningitis – 117.5 *[321.0]*
- Look for terms "in," "due to," or "with."
    - e.g., Polyneuropathy in rheumatoid arthritis – 714.0 *[357.1]*
- In most cases, manifestation codes will have in the code title "in diseases (or conditions) classified elsewhere." Codes with this title are a component of the etiology/manifestation combination. The code title indicates it is a manifestation code – e.g. *Acute myocarditis in diseases classified elsewhere.*
- The condition is in italics in the Tabular List followed by the instruction to "code first underlying disease." Not all conditions that may be manifestations are in italics. For example, an ulcer is not a true manifestation, since it is not always due to another condition and, therefore, may be coded alone and may be the primary diagnosis.
- "Code first underlying disease" indicates a manifestation code or tells you that the underlying condition must be coded before the manifestation. Even though a condition is the primary focus of care, it may have to be coded second. For example, when coding an ulcer that is a manifestation of diabetes and is the primary focus of care, the diabetes must be coded first – 250.8x, 707.1x. Another example is 357.3, Polyneuropathy in malignant disease, a manifestation code that directs you to code first the underlying disease (140.0-208.9). Therefore, when coding polyneuropathy due to malignant neoplasm of the spine, the neoplasm is coded first followed by the polyneuropathy – 170.2, 357.3.

Tip! *Code first does not mean code primary! Sequencing depends on the seriousness of the condition related to the plan of care. Regardless of where these are listed in the sequence of diagnoses, the etiology must always immediately precede the manifestation.*

Consider this scenario: Your patient has diabetic neuropathy and CHF.

- If diabetic neuropathy is the focus of care, you would code:

  M1020a Diabetes with neurological manifestations, 250.6x
  M1022b Polyneuropathy in diabetes, 357.2
  M1022c CHF, 428.0

- If CHF is the focus of care, then code:

  M1020a CHF, 428.0
  M1022b Diabetes with neurological manifestations, 250.6x
  M1022c Polyneuropathy in diabetes, 357.2

- Some examples of mandatory multiple coding are:
  - Retinopathy **due to** secondary diabetes
    - 249.5x, 362.01
  - Nephrosis **in** polyarteritis
    - 446.0, 581.81
  - Arthropathy **with** Reiter's Disease
    - 099.3, 711.1x

Tip! *The etiology/underlying condition is coded first, followed by the manifestation. They must be coded together!*

Tip! *Look up the manifestation in the Index.*

Multiple Coding for a Single Condition

In addition to the etiology/manifestation convention that requires two codes to fully describe a single condition that affects multiple body systems, there are other single conditions that require more than one code. "Use additional code" indicates that a secondary code should be added.

For example, for infections that are not included in Chapter 1, a secondary code from Category 041, Bacterial infection in conditions classified elsewhere and of unspecified site, may be required to identify the bacterial organism causing the infection. "Use additional code" will normally be found at the infectious disease code, indicating a need for the organism to be added as a secondary code, if known. For example, look at 599.0, Urinary tract infection, site not specified, and 997.62, Infection (chronic) of amputation stump.

The organism, if known, should be coded immediately following the infection.

In an etiology/manifestation situation, the additional code for the manifestation **must** be sequenced immediately after the etiology.

In other mandatory multiple coding situations, such as coding pressure ulcers (the site followed by the stage) and late effects (the residual condition followed by the late effect), the additional codes must also be sequenced next.

Otherwise, sequencing of the additional codes is discretionary. For example, the status code for the joint replaced or the aftercare code for attention to dressings may be sequenced after the numeric codes.

Tip! *Category 041 is provided to be used as an additional code to identify the bacterial agent in diseases classified elsewhere. Therefore, 041 codes are never a primary diagnosis.*

V Codes (V01- V91)

V codes are classifications of factors influencing health status and contact with health services. Since October 2003, home health agencies have been mandated to use V codes when a patient with a resolving disease or injury or a chronic condition encounters the health care system for specific aftercare or treatment, when circumstances or problems influence a person's health status but are not in themselves a current illness or injury, or to report reasons for encounters with health care providers.

If the patient has an acute condition relevant to the plan of care, continue to report the code for the acute condition. Whether it is listed as a primary or secondary diagnosis depends on the seriousness of the condition related to the care plan.

Some V codes are designated to be used as primary only, others can be assigned as secondary only, some as both. Pay attention to the designations in the coding manual indicating whether a V code can be primary only, secondary only, or either.

When is it appropriate to use V codes? You should use V codes when:

- they are more specific to the care being rendered than a medical diagnosis – e.g., attention to an ostomy
- a person has a resolving disease or injury and is admitted for:
  - surgical, orthopedic, or other routine aftercare – e.g., aftercare following a joint replacement
  - a person has a chronic, long-term condition and requires continuous care for a specific procedure – e.g., patient admitted for monthly catheter change due to neurogenic bladder resulting from MS
  - circumstances or problems influence a person's health status but are not in themselves a current illness or injury – e.g., amputation status or history of MRSA

V codes are **not** appropriate if:

- the patient has an acute condition, such as a complication of surgery or an exacerbation of a chronic condition
- a medical condition, such as pneumonia or a UTI, is unresolved
- they are <u>not</u> pertinent to the care being provided

How will you know when to use a V code? Ask yourself:

- Did the patient have surgery?
- Did the surgery resolve the condition?
- Was the patient treated for a condition that is now resolved?
- Was the patient admitted for a specific procedure?
- Is the patient going to receive therapy services only?
- Does the patient have circumstances or problems, either current or past, which may influence health status but are not in themselves a current illness or injury?

If you answered "yes" to one or more of the above, a V code may best describe the patient's condition and overall need for services.

How do you find V codes? Look in the Alphabetic Index for these key terms that are most often related to home care:

- Absence (main term for amputation status or organ removal)
- Admission for
- Aftercare
- Attention to
- Encounter for
- Fitting of
- History of
- Long-term
- Resistance
- Status (post)

V codes are organized by categories. The most commonly used categories in home care are history, status and aftercare.

History of (V10-V19)

History codes are used for persons with potential health hazards related to personal and family history.

Personal history codes explain a patient's past medical condition that is not receiving any treatment but that has the potential for recurrence and, therefore, may require continued monitoring – e.g., V12.61, Personal history of pneumonia. The exceptions to this general rule are Category V14, Personal history of allergy to medicinal agents, and subcategory V15.0, Allergy, other than to medicinal agents. A person who has had an allergic reaction to a substance or food in the past should always be considered allergic to the substance. Personal history codes are commonly used in home care.

Family history codes are for use when a patient has a family member who has had a particular disease that causes the patient to be at higher risk of also contracting the disease – e.g., V16.3, Family history of malignant breast neoplasm, may be used for a patient who has had prophylactic removal of breasts. Family history codes are seldom used in home care.

Many of the personal history codes are designated as primary or secondary. For example, all of the codes in Category V10 may be either.

Tip! *You will need to look in your coding manual to see which V codes may be coded as primary or secondary only.*

Status (V40-V49)

A status code is used for persons with a condition affecting their health status, which is not in itself a current illness or injury, or are a carrier of a disease, or have the sequelae or residual of a past disease or condition for which no care will be provided, or have another factor influencing their health status – e.g. the presence of prosthetic or mechanical devices resulting from past treatment.

A status code is informative because the status may affect the course of treatment and its outcome. This makes it distinct from a history code, which indicates that the patient no longer has the condition and requires no treatment for it.

Do **not** use a status code with a diagnosis code from one of the body system chapters, if the diagnosis code includes the information provided by the status code. For example, code V42.1, Heart transplant status, should not be used with code 996.83, Complications of transplanted heart. The status code does not provide additional information. The complication code indicates that the patient had a heart transplant.

Categories V42-V46 and subcategories V49.6 and V49.7 are for use only if there are no complications or malfunctions of the organ or tissue replaced, the amputation site, or the equipment on which the patient is dependent, except for V43.6. These are usually secondary codes, but there are exceptions. For example, V49.6 and V49.7 (upper and lower limb amputation status) codes may be primary or secondary, though it would be unusual to code them as primary.

Some examples of status codes that indicate a patient has the residual of a past condition or disease which may affect the course of treatment and its outcome are as follows:

- V43.6, Joint replaced – indicates the joint that was replaced and is the only exception to the rule that status codes are used when there are no complications. It is used with any joint replacement, even when complicated.

- V49.7, Lower limb amputation status – can be a new amputation or a long-standing amputation, as long as it is not complicated. If a complication exists such as an infected amputation stump, the complication code, 997.62, would be used and the status code would not.
- V49.83, Awaiting transplant status, (secondary diagnosis only), is sequenced after the condition requiring transplant.
- V44, Artificial opening status – indicates an artificial opening that does ***not*** require care by the home health agency (e.g., V44.1, Gastrostomy status).

Aftercare (V50-V59)

Aftercare codes, the most commonly used V codes in home care, are used when the initial treatment of a disease or injury has been performed and the patient requires continued care during the healing or recovery phase, or for the long-term consequences of the disease. They should **not** be used if treatment is directed at a current, acute disease or injury. Use the diagnosis code in these cases. *Exceptions to this rule are V58.0 Radiotherapy and V58.1x Chemotherapy*. These codes, which indicate "encounter or admission for," may only be assigned by the facility which is administering the therapy.

Certain aftercare V code categories need a secondary diagnosis code to describe the resolving condition or sequelae. For example, V58.4, Other aftercare following surgery, has a note stating that codes from this subcategory should be used in conjunction with other aftercare codes, such as a code for dressing changes or attention to an artificial opening, to fully identify the reason for the aftercare encounter. For others, the condition is inherent in the code title, such as V58.81, Fitting and adjustment of vascular catheter. Status V codes may be used with aftercare V codes to indicate the nature of the aftercare. For example, V54.81, Aftercare following joint replacement, gives the instruction to use an additional code to identify the joint replacement site (V43.60-V43.69).

Additional aftercare coding tips include:

- V53, Fitting and adjustment of other device should be used only if home health is providing the care. For example, V53.6, Urinary devices, is appropriate to use, whereas V53.3, Cardiac device, is not, unless it is being reprogrammed by the home health agency.

- V54, Other orthopedic aftercare
    - V54.0, Aftercare involving internal fixation device
        - Do **not** use this code, since this care is not provided by home health staff.
    - V54.1, Aftercare for healing traumatic fracture and V54.2, Aftercare for healing pathologic fracture
        - The 5th digit indicates the specific bone.
        - Use for all routine aftercare related to fractures, since HIPAA prohibits the use of all fracture codes, traumatic or pathologic, in M1020 and M1022 or as other diagnoses, whether or not active treatment was received.
        - The fracture codes are case-mix diagnoses, so they may be coded in M1024 and must be reported on the plan of care.
        - Exceptions to using V54.1 for traumatic fractures are if a joint replacement was done to repair the fracture (V54.81) or if there is a complication. If complicated, use the complication code.
    - V54.81, Aftercare following joint replacement
        - Use additional code to identify joint (V43.60-V43.69).
        - Use also when a joint replacement is performed to repair a trauma fracture.
        - Use as a primary diagnosis when nursing and therapy are treating a patient for aftercare associated with the joint replacement, when it is the focus of care.
        - Whether an abnormal gait is integral to lower extremity joint replacements has been a long-lingering question. According to the 2011 Q1 Coding Clinic, you ***may*** include a code for an abnormal gait, 781.2, when coding a patient who is receiving aftercare following a lower extremity joint replacement, if it provides additional necessary information. But, you are ***not*** required to. Whether or not to code it should be based on the discretion of the assessing clinician about what diagnoses best reflect the home care needs of the patient, in conjunction with the physician.

- V54.82, Aftercare following explantation of joint prosthesis
  - Use following explanation (removal) of a joint prosthesis – may be a staged procedure.
  - Use for joint prosthesis insertion following prior explantation of joint prosthesis
  - The status code for acquired absence of the joint (V88.2x) is used when the joint prosthesis was removed due to a complication, with or without the presence of an antibiotic cement spacer, and has ***not*** been replaced.
  - When the joint has been replaced, use V43.6x (joint replaced).

    Here are some examples:

    1. Patient had an infected hip joint prosthesis that was removed and an antibiotic-impregnated cement spacer was inserted. She had IV antibiotics in the hospital and continues on an oral antibiotic. She is scheduled to have surgery for a new joint prosthesis in 6 weeks.
       - M1020a 996.66 Infection due to internal joint prosthesis
       - M1022b V88.21 Acquired absence of hip joint
    2. Patient was admitted for PT following surgery for removal of a loose prosthetic knee joint, which was replaced with a new prosthesis.
       - M1020a V57.1 Admission for physical therapy
       - M1022b V54.82 Aftercare following explantation of joint prosthesis
       - M1022c V43.65 Knee joint replaced

Tip! *The status codes, V43.6x and V88.2x, do **not** need to be sequenced immediately following the aftercare codes.*

- V54.89, Other orthopedic aftercare
  - This code may be used when providing aftercare not included in the other V54 codes, such as for a healing fracture not specified as traumatic or pathologic, or when the code for

the underlying reason for an amputation does not fall within the range of "conditions classifiable to" for the aftercare following surgery codes (V58.4 and V58.7) – e.g., gangrene, 785.4. However, if gangrene is due to insufficient blood supply (e.g., peripheral vascular disease), V58.73, Aftercare following surgery of the circulatory system, may be used.

- V55, Attention to artificial openings
  - Use for artificial openings that receive care (feeding, cleansing, teaching) by the home health agency. For example, V55.5, Cystostomy, is used for care of a suprapubic catheter. If care is not being provided by the agency, look to the V44 status codes.

Tip! *When trying to decide between V44 and V55, ask who is providing the care.*

  - Do not use an attention to artificial opening code (V55) with the status code (V44) for the same artificial opening.
  - Do not use codes in the V55 category with status ostomy codes or when the ostomy is complicated.
  - The V55 codes are not meant for the care of a temporary artificial opening, such as a chest tube.
- V57, Care involving use of rehabilitation procedures
  - Therapy plays a major role under the Prospective Payment System. In 2008, a four-equation model for case-mix weight calculation, based on the timing of episodes and the number of therapy visits, was implemented. Medicare specifically states in M2200 (Therapy need) that the number of therapy visits must be "reasonable and necessary." Documentation in the medical record must support the therapy services being provided and the diagnoses selected!

    Codes from Category V57 may be used as a primary diagnosis only. Coding guidelines state "When the purpose for the admission/encounter is rehabilitation, sequence the appropriate V code from Category V57, Care involving use of rehabilitation procedures, as the principal/first-listed diagnosis. The code for which the service is being performed should be reported as an additional diagnosis. Only one code from V57 is required. Code V57.89, Other specified rehabilitation procedures, should be assigned if more than one type of rehabilitation is performed during a single encounter."

- For patients admitted to home care for therapy-only, report the appropriate V57 code as the primary diagnosis (M1020a) and the underlying condition (e.g., hemiparesis) as a secondary or other diagnosis (M1022b), immediately following the V code.
- If multiple therapies are being provided and no nursing, then V57.89 is sequenced first.
- V57 may be placed in M1020, but not in M1022 or M1024. Do ***not*** use this code, if nursing is being provided. However, if nursing is admitting the patient for therapy, then it is a therapy-only case, and V57 is the appropriate primary diagnosis.

• V58.3, Attention to dressings and sutures
  - Includes change or removal of wound packing, but not care of drains. Routine drain care is covered by the surgical aftercare code. Change or removal of drains is coded V58.49, but use this code only if the agency is changing or removing the drain.
  - Use only if the wound is ***not*** complicated – for routine care only!
  - Use as a secondary diagnosis, unless the only care being provided is the dressing change or removal of sutures or staples. This is rarely the case!

• V58.4, Other aftercare following surgery and V58.7, Aftercare following surgery to specified body systems, not elsewhere classified
  - Note "conditions classifiable to" when selecting code.
    e.g., aftercare following CABG
    Underlying condition is CAD – 414.01
    V58.73 Aftercare following surgery of the circulatory system
    – Conditions classifiable to 390-459
  - Use these codes when there is no complication.
  - Add other aftercare codes, such as a code for dressing change or attention to an artificial opening, to further specify the aftercare.

  - If the condition requiring surgery still exists, place it in M1022.
  - If the condition is resolved by surgery and no longer exists, do ***not*** place it in M1022.
  - V58.43, Aftercare following surgery for injury and trauma
  - Excludes aftercare for healing traumatic fracture (V54.10-V54.19)
- V58.6, Long-term (current) drug use
  - Use V58.6 as a secondary diagnosis only.
  - Assign V58.6 when the patient is expected to be on the medication long-term or the medication is used prophylactically (such as an anticoagulant). There is no definition for long-term, and long-term is different for different drugs.
  - Do not use for simple medication monitoring.
  - Use if the medication is pertinent to the plan of care or if coding guidelines indicate it should be used – e.g., insulin use in a Type 2 diabetic.
  - Do not assign V58.6 for medication being administered for a brief period of time to treat an acute illness or injury (such as a 7-day course of antibiotics to treat acute bronchitis).
- V58.81, Fitting and adjustment of vascular catheter
  - This code is appropriate for any IV or arterial line. It includes care to peripheral IVs, PICC lines, and all central venous access catheters.
  - For patients being seen for IV therapy, generally report the medical condition that requires the IV therapy first as the most acute condition (e.g., pneumonia).
  - If there is a complication of the vascular device, use codes 996.62, 999.31, 999.32, or 999.33 instead.
- V58.83, Encounter for therapeutic drug monitoring
  - Use additional code for any associated long-term (current) drug use (V58.61-V58.69).

- Sequence V58.83 as a secondary diagnosis and then the drug being monitored next – e.g., V58.83, V58.61.
- Do not use as the primary diagnosis for a home health patient, or for medication management, or filling medication boxes.
- Use only when assessing the effectiveness of a medication through lab data when the agency nurse obtains the blood.

Some V code facts to remember:

- V codes may be used in M1020 and M1022 but never in M1010, M1012, M1016, or M1024.
- V codes do not require a rating for the degree of symptom control.
- V codes are used for routine care only, with one exception – code the joint replaced with any joint replacement, even if complicated.

E Codes (E800-E999)

E codes, external causes of injury and poisoning, permit the classification of environmental events, circumstances and conditions as the cause of injury, poisoning and other adverse effects.

E codes may explain an injury of some kind. The injury may result from a number of causes including trauma due to violence, terrorism or accident, a medical misadventure, such as sponges left in during surgery, the wrong drug taken or given, or the correct drug, administered in the correct way, but still resulting in an adverse effect. E codes are intended to provide data for injury research and evaluation of injury prevention strategies. E codes identify the ***cause*** of the injury or poisoning, the ***intent*** (unintentional or accidental, or intentional, such as suicide or assault), and the ***place*** where the event occurred.

Coding guidelines instruct that an E code be assigned for the ***initial encounter*** of an injury, poisoning or adverse effect of drugs, not for subsequent treatment. The late effect E codes may be more appropriate in those situations. Late effect codes exist for injuries and poisonings but not for adverse effects of drugs, misadventures and surgical complications.

E codes are only *required* in home health to identify the causative substance for an adverse effect of therapeutic substances correctly prescribed and properly administered or for a poisoning.

E codes are ***not*** required to explain traumas in home health, but their use is not prohibited.

When reported, use the full range of E codes (E800-E999) to completely describe the cause, the intent and the place of occurrence, if applicable, for all injuries, poisonings, and adverse effects of drugs.

Assign as many E codes as necessary to fully explain each cause. If only one E code can be recorded, assign the E code most related to the principal diagnosis.

Use the Table of Drugs and Chemicals located in Volume 2, directly behind the Alphabetic Index, to identify poisoning states and external causes of adverse effects. Always refer back to Volume 1, the Tabular List, where E codes have their own section following the V codes.

- **Poisoning versus Adverse Effect**
  - A ***poisoning*** is the result of an accidental overdose, wrong substance given or taken in error, drug taken inadvertently, or intoxication. *Hint: The word "wrong" is a strong indication of a poisoning.*
  - Code the poisoning first, followed by the effect(s) of the poisoning, then the E code for the intent of the poisoning. If the reaction is due to a mixture of drugs and alcohol, use poisoning codes and E codes to describe both.
  - An example of poisoning is a patient with atrial fibrillation who misread the directions on the Lanoxin bottle and took twice the prescribed amount, resulting in bradycardia. Because the patient took the drug incorrectly, it is coded as a poisoning. Sequence the poisoning code for Lanoxin first, followed by the effect, bradycardia, the E code for the intent, which was accidental, and then atrial fibrillation, which is the reason for the medication. ***Note:*** *Lanoxin is not listed in the Table of Drugs and Chemicals, but Digoxin is. You must know that they are the same drug, or you must research another name for the drug.*

- An ***adverse effect*** is a pathologic manifestation due to ingestion or exposure to drugs or other chemical substances (e.g., dermatitis, hypersensitivity reaction, gastritis) when the correct substance is taken as directed (therapeutic use).
- Code the adverse effect(s), then the E code for therapeutic use (E930-E949). For example, a patient who is taking Coumadin correctly but has a GI bleed as a result, is experiencing an adverse effect of the Coumadin therapy. Code the adverse effect (GI bleed) first, then the E code for therapeutic use of Coumadin. Code, also, the reason the patient is taking Coumadin.

E codes also have their own Index in Volume 2 (Index to External Causes of Injury and Poisoning), following the Table of Drugs and Chemicals.

Tip! *Be familiar with the Table of Drugs and Chemicals in Volume 2 and its rules, as well as the E code Index in Volume 2 and the E code section in Volume 1.*

An E code provides supplementary information only. Therefore, it can never be the primary diagnosis (M1020). An E code may only be used as a secondary diagnosis (M1022 or other) and is ***not*** assigned a rating for the degree of symptom control.

Tip! *Never assign an E code to indicate the patient has fallen when there has been no injury. Instead, use V15.88, Personal history of fall.*

Pain Codes

The pain codes (338.0-338.4) may be used with other codes to provide more detail about acute or chronic pain and neoplasm-related pain.

If pain is not specified as acute or chronic, do not use category 338 codes except for:

- Post-thoracotomy pain
- Postoperative pain or
- Neoplasm-related pain

There is no time frame for chronic pain, but documentation must support its use.

Determine if the pain code provides additional information. If it does, determine whether it should be primary or secondary. If the pain code does ***not*** provide additional information, do ***not*** use it.

Assign a pain code as the primary diagnosis when the reason for the encounter is pain management and ***not*** management of the underlying condition.

When the definitive diagnosis is known and the focus of care is ***not*** pain management, do ***not*** assign 338. For example, a patient with rheumatoid arthritis should not be assigned a pain code, since pain is integral to the disease process.

When the reason for the pain is ***not*** known and the focus of care is ***not*** pain management, code the site of the pain first, followed by the pain code. For example, chronic shoulder pain is coded 719.41 (shoulder pain), 338.29 (other chronic pain).

Neoplasm-related pain can be classified as acute or chronic and both should be coded to 338.3. If pain management is the focus of care, assign this code as primary followed by the neoplasm code. In all other instances where neoplasm-related pain is documented and treated, code this as a secondary diagnosis.

Routine or expected postoperative pain should not be coded. Do ***not*** assign a pain code if there is a specific complication. Code the complication, unless the focus of care is pain management. Remember, pain management will always be the primary diagnosis, if it is the focus of care.

Central pain syndrome (338.0) and Chronic pain syndrome (338.4) must be specifically documented by the physician before a code can be assigned for them.

Tip! *Do not use a code from the acute or chronic categories, if the pain has not been documented as acute or chronic. An exception is post-procedural pain. The default code is acute.*

Coding Common Home Care Diagnoses

Fractures

Fracture codes, both pathologic (733.1x) and traumatic (categories 800-829) may only be used for the initial episode of care by the initial treating facility. The patient may have had surgical repair, an ER encounter, or evaluation and treatment by the physician only. The type of treatment does not matter.

All fractures are considered resolving for home care and, according to Health Insurance Portability and Accountability Act(HIPAA) regulations, they cannot be listed on the billing claim. This means that they cannot be placed in M1020, the M1022s, or as other diagnoses. Instead, use the *aftercare for healing fracture codes or aftercare following joint replacement*, if the treatment was a joint replacement. Regardless of the treatment rendered, the reason the patient is receiving home care is for aftercare, unless there is a complication. If complicated, assign the complication code.

Traumatic and pathologic fracture codes may be used in M1024 Column 3 for HHRG calculation and risk adjustment and also in M1010 and M1016, if appropriate.

Remember these things about fracture codes:

- Both traumatic fractures and pathologic fractures are case-mix diagnoses.
- When aftercare for healing fracture (V54.1x for traumatic fractures and V54.2x for pathologic fractures) is coded, the fracture code should be placed in M1024 Column 3 and on the plan of care.
- Use the personal history code for previous traumatic and pathologic fractures, when it is pertinent to the patient's care plan.

Coding Example:

A patient fractured the shaft of his tibia after falling at home. He now has a weight-bearing cast and is being admitted for physical therapy for transfer and gait training, and nursing for assessment and management of his acute pain.

Because the patient is receiving both nursing and therapy in the aftercare for his fracture, use V54.16 for the primary diagnosis. The underlying diagnosis for that V code is the fracture, so code 823.20, fracture of the tibia shaft, in M1024 Column 3. *Do NOT code the fracture in M1022 or as another diagnosis, since that will violate HIPAA regulations and official coding guidelines.* The fracture code must also be placed on the plan of care. In this situation, code 338.11, Acute pain due to trauma, should be listed in M1022c.

Note: *The general consensus among coding experts is that abnormality of gait is integral to lower extremity fractures and, therefore, it is not necessary to code 781.2.*

Tip! *Never code the acute fracture, whether traumatic or pathologic, as a primary or secondary diagnosis!*

Diabetes Mellitus (Category 250)

Knowing some facts about diabetes and following a few simple rules can make diabetes coding less complicated.

Diabetes is a comorbidity that should always be coded. It is a case-mix diagnosis worth 1-13 points depending on whether it is the primary or secondary diagnosis, the episode timing (early or later), and the number of therapy visits. Points will only be given once, either primary or secondary, for the same encounter.

The terms insulin dependent (IDDM) and non-insulin dependent (NIDDM) no longer exist. Type 1 is still known as juvenile diabetes. Only 5-10% of diabetics are Type 1. Type 1 diabetics have no ability to produce insulin and are, therefore, dependent on insulin for survival. The fact that a diabetic needs insulin does not make that person Type 1. Type 2, or unspecified type diabetes, can develop at any age and is, by far, the most prevalent (90%-95%) type of diabetes. Type 2 diabetics produce insulin but may need additional insulin to control their blood sugar. If the patient is Type 2 and on insulin, add V58.67, Long-term (current) use of insulin.

Tip! *V58.67 is not necessary for Type 1 diabetes, since the use of insulin is always required.*

Diabetes always requires 5 digits – 250.xx

- 250 = Diabetes
- 4th digit = complication or manifestation
- 5th digit = type and control

4th Digit – Complication or Manifestation

- The 4th digit identifies a complication of diabetes – metabolic complication or manifestation.
- Never code the 4th digit '0' when also coding a manifestation of diabetes.
- If a manifestation, the diabetes must be coded first, even if the manifestation is the focus of care – e.g., diabetic ulcer.
- Multiple diabetic complications/manifestations may be coded in order to fully describe the patient's condition.
- Even though diabetes may be the underlying cause of the problem, the only manifestations that can be assumed are gangrene and osteomyelitis, unless the physician links them to another cause. Others need physician documentation. If the documentation does not include "caused by," "as a result of," "due to," "diabetic" (e.g., diabetic ESRD), "with" (e.g., diabetes with neuropathy) or "secondary to," then no relationship is assumed.
- If there is no supporting documentation, obtain verification from the physician whether the patient has a manifestation of the diabetes or two separate comorbidities.

Tip! *Diabetes with loss of protective sensation (LOPS) is coded as diabetic polyneuropathy.*

5th Digit – Type and Control

- Do not consider insulin use as an indicator for choosing the 5th digit.
- When the type of diabetes is not documented, default to Type 2, unspecified type.
- Use 5th digits '0' (type 2 or unspecified type – not stated as uncontrolled) or '2' (type 2 or unspecified type – uncontrolled), unless the physician designates that the patient has Type 1 or juvenile diabetes.

- Use 5th digits '1' (type 1 or juvenile type – not stated as uncontrolled) or '3' (Type 1 or juvenile type – uncontrolled) for patients with documented Type 1 or juvenile diabetes.
- Do not code diabetes as "uncontrolled" unless the physician specifically documents or states that it is "uncontrolled" or "out of control." You cannot assume that diabetes is uncontrolled based on terms like "poorly controlled," "brittle," or "resistant," recent hospitalization, or variation in blood sugars.
- A '0' or '1' as the 5th digit does not indicate that the diabetes is controlled, just that the physician did not say that the diabetes is uncontrolled. The presence of complications or manifestations does not indicate "uncontrolled."
- If unsure, consult the physician and document!

More Diabetes Coding Tips:

- If the patient has diabetes without mention of a complication, code 250.0x.
- Diabetic macular edema and osteomyelitis require three codes. Be sure to look up all codes and follow the instructions!
- A pressure ulcer is ***not*** a manifestation of diabetes.
- Diabetic ulcers are coded with a 4th digit of '8' unless the physician specifically documents a link between the ulcer and the neurological (250.6x) or peripheral vascular (250.7x) complications.
- If a V code is assigned as the primary diagnosis in M1020 following surgery due to a diabetic manifestation, such as an amputation, be sure to report the diabetes and manifestation, if they still exist, in M1022b and M1022c to capture the primary case-mix points. If the manifestation no longer exists, list the diabetes in M1022b but not the manifestation.

Secondary Diabetes Mellitus (Category 249)

Category 249, Secondary diabetes mellitus, identifies diabetes caused by another condition or event (e.g., cystic fibrosis, malignant neoplasm of pancreas, adverse effect of a drug, or poisoning).

Category 249 also requires 5 digits. Like category 250, the 4th digit identifies the complication or manifestation. However, the 5th digit indicates the control only. A 5th digit of '0' indicates "not stated as uncontrolled or unspecified" and '1' indicates "uncontrolled."

Use an additional code to identify any associated insulin use (V58.67).

For example, diabetic nephrosis due to steroid use is coded 249.4x (Secondary diabetes mellitus with renal manifestations) immediately followed by 581.81 (Diabetic nephrosis), then E932.0 (Adverse effect of steroids).

Coding Examples:

According to a referral, the patient has gangrenous toes and diabetes. You may assume the gangrene is a manifestation of the diabetes and code it as such, coding first 250.70, Diabetes with peripheral circulatory disorders, followed by 785.4, Gangrene.

What if the referral from the physician states that the patient has a gangrenous pressure ulcer on the heel and diabetes? You cannot assume the gangrene is a manifestation of the diabetes, because the gangrene is in the pressure ulcer, which is not a manifestation of diabetes. The physician documentation links the gangrene to the pressure ulcer. Code the pressure ulcer on the heel first, 707.07, then code the pressure ulcer stage, the gangrene, 785.4, and the diabetes with the 4th digit '0,' meaning it has no manifestations or complications, 250.00.

In both examples, a 5th digit of '0' (type 2 or unspecified type, not stated as uncontrolled) is assigned since there is no documentation stating the type or that it is uncontrolled.

Cerebrovascular Accident (CVA)

Patients discharged from an inpatient facility following a "stroke" are often admitted to home care for rehabilitation. According to ICD-9-CM guidelines, Category 434 for the acute CVA should be reserved for the inpatient facility. Acute CVA is ***not*** an appropriate diagnosis for home health.

Per CMS, "The conditions in categories 430-437 identify the cause of the initial onset of an acute stroke and must not be assigned in the home health setting." However, codes from these categories may be assigned in limited circumstances, as when there has been no cerebral infarct (e.g., 433.10, Carotid stenosis without mention of cerebral infarction).

Late effects of cerebrovascular disease, Category 438, are to be assigned for conditions occurring any time after the onset of an acute stroke or TIA when there are neurologic deficits that persist.

The 438 codes are case-mix diagnoses that are worth different point values depending on combinations with other diagnoses or specific OASIS data elements, the episode timing (early or later episode), and the number of therapy visits.

V12.54, Personal history of transient ischemic attack (TIA), and cerebral infarction without residual deficits, is to be assigned when there are no residuals or neurologic deficits present.

Tip! *Category 434 should never be used when the documentation states stroke or CVA!*

Late Effects of Cerebrovascular Disease

Use Category 438, Late effects of cerebrovascular disease, for conditions occurring any time after the onset of an acute stroke or TIA when there are neurologic deficits that persist after the initial onset of conditions classifiable to 430-437. The neurologic deficits may be present from the onset or may arise at any time after the onset of the CVA or TIA.

Some 438 codes are combination codes that include the residual deficit within the code – e.g., 438.0 (Cognitive deficits) – and do not require another code. Others require a second code to identify the deficit – e.g., 438.7 (Disturbances of vision).

Late effect codes in Category 438 require 4 or 5 digits.

- 4th digit identifies the residual condition
- 5th digit, if required, further describes the condition
- Examples:
  - Hemiplegia, dominant side – 438.21
  - Muscle weakness due to CVA – 438.89, 728.87

Tip! *Many 438 codes are combination codes and do not require a second code.*

Coding Example:

A patient has hemiplegia (dominant side) and dysphagia resulting from a CVA, and has nursing, PT and OT services ordered. Assign codes 438.21 for late effect CVA with hemiplegia affecting dominant side, 438.82 for late effect dysphagia and, also, 787.20 for unspecified dysphagia. Code 438.82 instructs to use an additional code to identify the type of dysphagia (787.20-787.29), if known. If the type is unknown, assign 787.20 for unspecified type.

Tip! *When coding hemipelgia, a 5th digit of '0' (unspecified side) should not be assigned. The side that is affected should be determined during the assessment for more specificity in describing the patient's condition.*

Hypertensive Heart Disease and Heart Failure

The Hypertension Table, found in the Alphabetic Index, contains a complete listing of all conditions due to or associated with hypertension, and classifies them according to the type: Malignant, Benign or Unspecified.

Essential hypertension (401), the most common form, is used to describe hypertension where an underlying cause has not been identified. When an underlying cause is identified, this is secondary hypertension (405).

Physicians typically do not document the type of hypertension as benign or malignant, which is needed to code these types. Unspecified hypertension NOS is coded 401.9. Do not assume that hypertension is benign or malignant without physician documentation.

Certain heart conditions are assigned to Category 402, Hypertensive heart disease, when the heart disease is linked to hypertension – e.g., a causal relationship is stated (due to hypertension) or implied (hypertensive). A cause-and-effect relationship cannot be assumed.

Hypertension is coded before the heart condition. Use an additional code from Category 428 to identify the type of heart failure in those patients with documented heart failure. More than one code from Category 428 may be assigned if the patient has more than one type of heart failure, such as systolic or diastolic failure and congestive heart failure. Without a stated causal relationship, these conditions are coded separately. Look at the wording in the diagnostic statement. If the documentation states CHF and/with HTN, code each condition separately – 428.0, 401.9 – according to the seriousness of the condition related to the care plan.

When a patient has hypertension and chronic kidney disease (CKD) or renal sclerosis, it is assumed that there is a cause-and-effect relationship. Assign a code from category 403 when a condition classified to 585 (CKD) or 587 (Renal sclerosis) are present with hypertension. The 5th digit indicates the stage of chronic kidney disease. The specific stage of CKD (585.1-585.9) must also be coded. If the patient has hypertension and renal sclerosis, assign the 5th digit of '0' and code renal sclerosis.

Tip! *Chronic kidney disease requiring dialysis is coded as end stage renal disease (ESRD) – 585.6. Also code V45.11, Renal dialysis status.*

When both hypertensive heart disease and hypertensive chronic kidney disease exist, assume a causal relationship and assign only one code from Category 404, Hypertensive heart and chronic kidney disease.

If heart failure is present, at least two codes are required. Code hypertensive heart disease first (Category 402 or 404). Use additional code(s) to identify the type(s) of heart failure (428.0-428.43), if known.

Heart failure (Category 428) is one of the most common diagnoses in home care. Be careful – the term "heart failure" is ***not*** interchangeable with "congestive heart failure." Many patients with heart failure do not manifest pulmonary or systemic congestion. If not documented, the physician must be queried as to the type – systolic, diastolic, combined systolic and diastolic, or congestive heart failure.

Remember these additional tips when coding heart failure:

- If there is more than one type of heart failure, code them all (e.g., diastolic heart failure and congestive heart failure – 428.30, 428.0).
- CHF includes right heart failure secondary to left heart failure – do ***not*** code 428.0 (CHF) and 428.1 (Left heart failure) separately.
    - CHF takes precedence

    - Excludes fluid overload (276.6x)
- All codes for heart failure include any associated pulmonary edema, so it is ***not*** necessary to code both. For example, you would ***not*** code 428.0 and 514.

Coding Examples:

CHF due to hypertension – 402.91, 428.0

Use Category 402 when the documentation states a cause-and-effect relationship. Remember, "due to" indicates the cause of a condition – code the cause first.

CHF with hypertension – 428.0, 401.9

There is no causal relationship. Remember, "with" indicates the condition is secondary, in this situation. Sequence the diagnoses according to their seriousness related to the care plan.

CHF with pulmonary edema and left heart failure – 428.0

CHF includes any left-sided failure that is present. Codes 428.0 and 428.1 are not assigned together– 428.0 takes precedence. All codes for heart failure include any associated pulmonary edema.

Acute exacerbation of chronic diastolic heart failure with CHF – 428.33, 428.0

When the documentation states both acute and chronic heart failure, use the combination code – acute on chronic. If the patient has both acute and chronic heart failure, the acute condition is always sequenced first. CHF is considered chronic.

CHF due to systolic heart failure due to hypertension – 402.91, 428.20, 428.0

In this type of scenario, start at the end of the diagnostic statement. "Due to" links the heart failure to the hypertension. The hypertension code is sequenced first, then systolic heart failure, and then CHF.

Tip! *Patients with heart failure will often develop blisters caused by excessive edema, which is known as weeping edema. These are coded as nontraumatic blisters – 709.8.*

Myocardial Infarction (MI)

A myocardial infarction is considered "acute" for a period of eight weeks. Use Category 410 when the infarction occurred within the past eight weeks. The 4th digit identifies the site of the infarct. The 5th digit is for the episode of care. Home care will always use '2' (subsequent episode of care) as the 5th digit, if services are ordered within eight weeks post-MI (e.g., 410.92, Acute myocardial infarction NOS, unspecified site, subsequent episode of care).

Assign '1' (first episode of care) as the 5th digit in M1010 and M1016, if appropriate. If a myocardial infarction is specified as "old" (greater than eight weeks after the acute attack), or "healed" and the patient currently has no symptoms, assign code 412, Old myocardial infarction.

If a myocardial infarction occurred greater than eight weeks prior to the initiation of home care or upon recertification and the patient is having continued symptoms, such as angina, assign code 414.8, Other specified forms of chronic ischemic heart disease.

Coronary artery disease (CAD) should also be coded since it is pertinent to the care plan and is a comorbidity that should always be reported. Assign 414.00 when the documentation states CAD but does not specify which coronary arteries are involved. Code 414.01 indicates CAD in a patient who has never had a bypass.

Coding Example:

Code myocardial infarction of the inferolateral wall that occurred 1½ weeks ago.

- 410.22

What code will you place in M1010?

- 410.21

What will you code on the Recertification POC?

- 412 – no symptoms
- 414.8 – with symptoms

Tip! *The 5th digit must always be a '2' for home care when coding a myocardial infarction in order to earn the case-mix points.*

COPD (490-496)

Chronic obstructive pulmonary disease (COPD) is an irreversible obstruction of the airways and is associated with chronic asthma, chronic obstructive bronchitis and emphysema. Category 496, Chronic airway obstruction, not elsewhere classified, which includes COPD, has an instructional note stating that this code is ***not*** to be used with any code from categories 491-493. Category 496 is a general code that is ***not*** reported when specific information as to the type of COPD, such as chronic asthma, is available.

Respiratory insufficiency (518.82) is an integral part of COPD and would ***not*** be reported as an additional code.

Acute exacerbation is the worsening of a chronic condition. Exacerbation of COPD or decompensated COPD, also known as end-stage, is coded 491.21, Obstructive chronic bronchitis with acute exacerbation. A coding guideline states "If a medical record documents COPD with acute exacerbation without mention of acute bronchitis, only code 491.21 should be assigned."

Since COPD overlaps with asthma, emphysema, and/or bronchitis, there are many variations on how these conditions are documented. Code selection must be based on the terms as documented! There are many instructional notes under the different COPD subcategories and codes. It is important to review all the documentation to assure correct code assignment. Examples of codes that are not reported together are listed in notes under the codes.

When the documentation links asthma and COPD, report a code from category 493 (asthma). A note under code 493.2 (chronic obstructive asthma) excludes chronic obstructive bronchitis (491.20-491.22) and acute bronchitis (466).

When the documentation links acute bronchitis and COPD, report code 491.22 (obstructive chronic bronchitis with acute bronchitis). A note under code 466 (acute bronchitis) excludes this code. Therefore, only 491.22 is reported.

When COPD with emphysema is documented, report a code from category 492 (emphysema). A note under code 492.8 (other emphysema) excludes emphysema with chronic bronchitis (491.20-491.22).

Additional coding instructions are in the Coding Guidelines in the front of the coding manual, in Chapter-Specific guidance at the beginning of Chapter 8 and in Coding Tips under the codes in the Tabular List.

Tip! *Chronic COPD is coded 496, not 491.20, Obstructive chronic bronchitis without exacerbation.*

Embolism and Thrombosis

A pulmonary embolism (415.1x) is a closure of the pulmonary artery or branch due to thrombosis (blood clot).

Most patients are treated with anticoagulant therapy for an acute embolism for 3-6 months. Do not code chronic pulmonary embolism (416.2), unless the physician documents that it is chronic. Most pulmonary emboli do not cause chronic disease. If treatment persists longer than 3-6 months after the acute pulmonary embolism, verify with the physician whether chronic disease is being treated or if the patient is being treated prophylactically.

If not chronic, code V12.55 for history of pulmonary embolism.

Venous embolism and thrombosis of the lower and upper extremities (category 453) are coded as acute, unless physician documentation indicates chronic.

Neoplasms (140-239)

A neoplasm is any new and abnormal growth of tissue in which the growth is uncontrolled and progressive. Malignant neoplasms are distinguished from benign ones in that they have the properties of invasion and metastasis.

The Neoplasm Table, located in the Alphabetic Index, lists the codes for neoplasms by anatomical site. For each site, there are six possible codes according to whether the neoplasm is malignant – primary, secondary, cancer in situ – benign, uncertain, or unspecified. If malignant, any secondary (metastatic) sites should be determined. Look for terms such as primary site, metastasis (or "mets"), metastasis to, and metastasis from.

The description of the neoplasm will often indicate which of the six columns is appropriate – e.g., malignant melanoma of skin, benign fibroadenoma of breast, carcinoma in situ of cervix uteri. Where such descriptors are **not** present, the Alphabetic Index should be consulted first, which is where you will find guidance as to the appropriate column – e.g., Mesonephroma – *see also* Neoplasm, by site, malignant. However, the guidance in the Index can be overridden if one of the descriptors is present. For example, malignant adenoma of the colon is coded 153.9 and ***not*** 211.3, as the adjective "malignant" overrides the Index entry "Adenoma – see also Neoplasm, by site, benign."

Sites marked with an asterisk (e.g., face NEC*) should be classified to malignant neoplasm of the skin of these sites, if the variety of neoplasm is a squamous cell or an epidermoid carcinoma, and to benign neoplasm of the skin of these sites, if the variety of neoplasm is a papilloma (any type). For example, the code for papilloma of the leg is 216.7 (benign neoplasm of the skin – leg).

Tip! *Understand how to use the Neoplasm Table. Read the guidance at the top of the Table. Verify the code in the Tabular List. Always read and adhere to the instructional notes.*

Sequencing Neoplasms

The first step in sequencing neoplasms is to determine the focus of care. The primary site is not always the primary focus of care. Code the location being treated first. It may be the primary or secondary site. If the treatment is directed at the primary malignancy, code it as the principal diagnosis. If the treatment is directed at the secondary site only, code the secondary neoplasm as the principal diagnosis, even though the primary malignancy may still be present.

If the treatment is directed to both the primary and secondary sites, code the primary malignant site as the principal diagnosis. If the diagnostic statement does not indicate primary or secondary, assume primary, except for the following: bone, brain, diaphragm, heart, liver, lymph nodes, mediastinum, meninges, peritoneum, pleura, retroperitoneum, spinal cord, which are usually secondary sites, and sites classified to Category 195. If uncertain, consult with the physician. If the site of malignancy is unknown, assign a code from Category 199, Malignant neoplasm without specification of site.

If management of the neoplasm-related pain is the primary focus of care, assign 338.3, Neoplasm-related pain, as the principal diagnosis.

The primary focus may be a numeric code or a V code. Assign V58.42, Aftercare following surgery for neoplasm, when the reason for surgery is classifiable to codes 140-239. Use additional aftercare codes to fully describe the reason for aftercare – e.g., V55.3, Attention to colostomy, or V58.31, Attention to surgical dressing.

If the patient needs further treatment, or if unknown, report the numeric code for the neoplasm in M1022. If treatment eradicated the malignancy and no further treatment is needed, assign a code from Category V10, personal history of malignant neoplasm, in M1022 – e.g., V10.85, Personal history of malignant brain neoplasm or V12.41, Personal history of benign neoplasm of the brain (only history code for benign neoplasm).

Most malignant neoplasms, including secondary, and some benign ones, are case-mix diagnoses when listed as the primary <u>or</u> secondary diagnosis. Malignant and benign neoplasms of the brain, spinal cord, and meninges are in the Neuro 1 case-mix diagnosis group.

Coding Example:

Your patient, diagnosed with metastasis from the lung to the esophagus, was admitted to home care following surgery to the esophagus. Nursing care includes assessment, dressing changes, diet teaching and monitoring of meds. The patient is still receiving treatment of the esophagus site. The primary site was resected and there are no current symptoms and no further treatment is needed.

M1020a	V58.42	Aftercare following surgery for neoplasm
M1022b	197.8	Secondary site respiratory and digestive systems
M1022c	V58.31	Attention to surgical dressings
M1022d	V10.11	Personal history malignant neoplasm of lung

- If resolved, the neoplasm ***may*** be reported in M1024, but no case-mix points will be earned. The secondary neoplasm of the esophagus is unresolved, so it would ***not*** be listed in M1024 across from the V code in M1020a. The same neoplasm would be the reason for the dressing changes, so it would not be placed in

M1024 across from M1022c. Malignant neoplasm of the lung is the underlying condition for the history code, but it is not necessary to code it in M1024 across from the V code in M1022d, since no case-mix points would be earned for the V10 history code.

Coding and Sequencing of Complications due to Malignancy

Per coding guidelines, when the admission/encounter is for management of anemia associated with the malignancy or associated with chemotherapy, immunotherapy or radiotherapy, and the treatment is only for anemia, the appropriate anemia code is designated as the principal diagnosis and is followed by the appropriate code(s) for the malignancy.

The anemia code may also be used as a secondary code if the patient has anemia due to neoplastic disease and is being treated for the malignancy.

Anemia in neoplastic disease, 285.22, and Antineoplastic chemotherapy induced anemia, 285.3, may both be coded, if both are documented.

When the admission/encounter is for management of dehydration due to the malignancy or therapy, or a combination of both, and only the dehydration is being treated (intravenous rehydration) the dehydration is sequenced first, followed by the code(s) for the malignancy. If dehydration is due to chemotherapy, dehydration is sequenced first, then E933.1, adverse effect of antineoplastic drugs given therapeutically, and then the code(s) for the malignancy.

When the admission/encounter is for treatment of a complication resulting from a surgical procedure, designate the complication as the principal diagnosis, if treatment is directed at resolving the complication. Remember, complications must be verified by the physician!

If the purpose of the admission/encounter is solely for administration of chemotherapy (V58.11) or immunotherapy (V58.12), code the antineoplastic therapy as the principal diagnosis. If the patient receives more than one of these therapies during the same admission, both of these codes may be assigned, in any sequence. The malignancy for which the therapy is being administered should be listed as a secondary diagnosis.

If the patient develops complications, such as uncontrolled nausea and vomiting or dehydration, code the V58.1 code for the antineoplastic therapy as the principal diagnosis followed by the code(s) for the complication(s) and the malignancy.

Tip! *V58.1 codes can only be assigned by the facility administering the antineoplastic therapy.*

Symptoms, signs and ill-defined conditions listed in Chapter 16 characteristic of, or associated with, an existing primary or secondary site malignancy cannot be used to replace the malignancy as the principal diagnosis, regardless of the number of admissions or encounters for treatment and care of the neoplasm. Code the neoplasm first and then the symptoms.

A malignant neoplasm of a transplanted organ should be coded as a transplant complication. Assign first the appropriate code from subcategory 996.8, Complications of transplanted organ, followed by code 199.2, Malignant neoplasm associated with transplanted organ. Use an additional code for the specific malignancy. For example, a malignant neoplasm in a transplanted kidney is coded:

M1020a 996.81 Complications of transplanted organ, kidney
M1022b 199.2 Malignancy associated with organ transplant
M1022c 189.0 Malignant neoplasm of kidney

Symptom Coding

Symptom codes, found in Chapter 16 of Volume 1 – Signs, Symptoms and Ill-Defined Conditions (780-799) – describe patient problems, not diseases. While Chapter 16 codes can be assigned as the principal diagnosis in M1020, it is preferable to code a definitive diagnosis, if determined, for both coding accuracy and risk adjustment. This may also impact reimbursement.

Code only "confirmed" diagnoses. Do ***not*** code "rule out," "suspected," or "probable" diagnoses. If there is no definitive diagnosis, coding the symptom(s) may be the only option.

Code the disease when there is a new diagnosis, exacerbation of an existing diagnosis, or when addressing multiple aspects of the disease process, such as comprehensive disease management of a neuro patient (e.g., CVA, MS, Parkinson's). It is not necessary that multiple disciplines be involved in order to code the disease. However, the plan of care and documentation must reflect management of the disease, not just the symptom.

If a symptom is integral to the condition, part of the disease process itself, do not code it. Some examples include:

- dependent and pulmonary edema in CHF
- dyspnea in COPD or heart failure
- muscle weakness and gait abnormality in hemiplegia
- gait abnormality in low back pain
- joint stiffness in osteoarthritis
- jaundice in hepatitis

If you are unsure whether a symptom is integral to the disease process, refer to medical resources to determine the symptomology of the condition you are coding.

Code the symptom when:

- There is no definitive diagnosis
    - e.g., Abdominal pain when the etiology is unknown
- A diagnosis has been resolved
    - e.g., Shortness of breath following pneumonia no longer being treated
- The symptom is not always part of the condition
    - e.g., Gait abnormality in a patient with Alzheimer's
- Caring for one aspect of a chronic condition
    - e.g., Urinary incontinence in a patient with multiple sclerosis
- The code book instructs you to code the symptom
    - e.g., Urinary retention in a patient with hypertrophy of the prostate (see 600.01 and 600.21)

Keep in mind the proximate diagnosis versus the underlying condition rule. You must determine whether the underlying condition or the resulting condition is the primary focus of care and assign that as your primary diagnosis.

Disease versus Symptom Example

You admit a patient with Alzheimer's dementia who is having an acute exacerbation with increased dementia, wandering, combativeness, gait and balance problems, as well as ADL deficits. She also has frequent episodes of inappropriate laughing and crying, which the physician diagnosed as Pseudobulbar affect, a result of her Alzheimer's. She has new and changed medications. SN is ordered for neuro assessment and monitoring of her medication regimen. She will also receive PT for gait training and OT for ADL management.

M1020a	331.0	Alzheimer's Disease
M1022b	294.11	Dementia with behavioral disturbance
M1022c	310.81	Pseudobulbar affect
M1022d	781.2	Abnormality of gait
M1022e	V40.31	Wandering in conditions classified elsewhere

Note: *Since multiple aspects of the disease process are being addressed, code Alzheimer's disease as the primary diagnosis. The diagnosis of "Alzheimer's dementia" makes this an etiology/manifestation situation. Therefore, 294.11, a manifestation code, is listed immediately after the etiology. If the dementia was* ***not*** *noted as being due to Alzheimer's, 294.21, Dementia, unspecified, with behavioral disturbance, would be coded instead. Pseudobulbar affect is an involuntary emotional expression disorder, which may occur in patients with neurological conditions such as Alzheimer's, CVA, traumatic brain injury, or multiple sclerosis. Abnormality of gait is* ***not*** *integral to Alzheimer's, so this symptom should be coded as a secondary diagnosis and will support the need for PT. Wandering is* ***not*** *integral to dementia, so V40.31 should be reported. It is not necessary that this code be sequenced immediately after the dementia.*

Symptom versus Disease Example

You recertified a patient with MS whose only skilled service is a monthly Foley catheter change due to urinary retention. She also needs aide services 3x/week to assist with bathing and ADLs.

M1020a	V53.6	Fitting and adjustment of urinary catheter
M1022b	788.20	Retention of urine
M1022c	340	Multiple sclerosis

Note: *Since only one aspect of care is being addressed, that is the primary diagnosis. The aide visits are not considered, since they are unskilled. The underlying condition is the urinary retention caused by the multiple sclerosis, but these are not the focus of care. Therefore, they are coded as secondary diagnoses. No diagnosis may be placed in M1024, since urinary retention is not a case-mix diagnosis and it is not resolved. Remember, only acute fracture codes earn case-mix points in M1024!*

Abnormality of Gait versus Difficulty in Walking

Abnormality of Gait – 781.2

Abnormality of gait, 781.2, is found in Chapter 16 – Symptoms, Signs and Ill-Defined Conditions. It applies to gait that is ataxic, paralytic, spastic or staggering, which infers a neurological problem. Therefore, use abnormality of gait for neuro problems such as CVA, MS, ALS (Amyotrophic lateral sclerosis), Parkinson's, and Alzheimer's. CMS has indicated that it is permissible to use this code for post-op orthopedic patients. It may also be used for falls of unknown etiology.

If integral to a condition, such as hemiplegia or low back pain, abnormality of gait, a symptom, should ***not*** be coded.

Research has been done to determine if a gait abnormality is integral to Parkinson's, and it has been determined that it is.

This code is a case-mix diagnosis but will gain points only if the patient has a pressure ulcer, is in the first or second adjacent episode of care, and requires 13 or fewer therapy visits.

> **Tip!** *Just because the therapist or physician mentions "gait abnormality," it does not mean that it is the right coding diagnosis. Clinicians should investigate the cause of the gait problem.*

Difficulty in Walking – 719.7

Difficulty in walking, 719.7, is found in Chapter 13 – Diseases of the Musculoskeletal System & Connective Tissue – under the category "Other and unspecified disorders of joint." It infers a relationship to "joint disorders" as the etiology of the problem. Difficulty in walking is used when there is a chronic condition involving the bone or joint and when there has been no surgical intervention, manipulation or repair of the joint or bone. Use difficulty in walking for arthritic patients who have not had surgery and for any other gait deficit related to problems in lower-extremity joints, such as loose bodies, synovitis, effusion or stiffness.

Wounds

To code wounds accurately, it is imperative to determine the specific type of wound – abrasion, skin tear, laceration, surgical, burn, ulcer – diabetic, stasis, arterial, pressure, or chronic – and the origin. If it is a surgical wound, you need to know the disease/condition for which the procedure was performed.

Assign the complication code, if documentation supports the following:

- Infection
  - Use additional code to identify organism, if known
- Delayed healing
- Delayed treatment
- Dehiscence
- Foreign body

A 4th digit is often required to indicate the presence or absence of a complication. A 5th digit specifies the location of the wound.

e.g., 881.10 – Open wound, complicated, forearm

A **pressure ulcer** is defined as any lesion caused by unrelieved pressure resulting in tissue hypoxia and damage to the underlying tissue. Pressure ulcers most often occur over bony prominences and can also result from friction or shearing. A pressure ulcer may present as a serous-filled blister, which is a Stage II. A blood-filled blister is a deep tissue injury (DTI) and is coded as an unstageable pressure ulcer.

Coding pressure ulcers requires two codes for each ulcer: one for the site, and one for the stage. All of these codes are five-digit codes. First, code the site: 707.01-707.09. Then, code the stage immediately following the site: 707.20-707.25.

Code all pressure ulcers, including Stage I. If there is more than one ulcer, code them in the order of seriousness related to the care plan. Remember, you can only code the same site and the same stage once.

Tip! *Do not code 707.00, "unspecified site." If there is a documented wound, the site must be known!*

Tip! *A pressure ulcer on the ischial tuberosity is coded as buttock, 707.05.*

Remember, a pressure ulcer is ***not*** a manifestation of diabetes. If the physician documents that a diabetic patient has a "gangrenous pressure ulcer," the gangrene is linked to the pressure ulcer and ***not*** to the diabetes. Note in the Index Gangrene, decubital (*see also Ulcer, pressure)* 707.00 *[785.4].* This identifies the gangrene as a manifestation and the pressure ulcer as the etiology.

A pressure ulcer that is surgically debrided or covered with a skin graft remains a pressure ulcer and is ***not*** a surgical wound. These are considered treatments, not surgery. However, a muscle flap, skin advancement flap or rotational flap performed to surgically replace a pressure ulcer is a surgical wound but is coded as an unstageable pressure ulcer.

Other ulcers – chronic, arterial and stasis – require 4 or 5 digits to specify the site (707.10-707.19 and 707.8). Although found in the Alphabetic Index as a manifestation of other diseases, 707.1x, Ulcer of lower limbs, except pressure ulcer, may be coded without its underlying cause, if unknown. If the underlying cause is known, sequence the underlying cause before the ulcer code – e.g., chronic venous HTN with ulcer – 459.31, 707.1x. More than one 707.1x code may be used depending on the number of ulcers, cause, and location on the lower limb.

Tip! *Remember, diabetic ulcers are NOT pressure ulcers, and, depending on the etiology, they may be coded to 249.6x/250.6x, 249.7x/250.7x,or 249.8x/250.8x.*

If the type of ulcer has not been documented, consult the physician.

Note: *Certain skin conditions such as abscesses, cellulitis, and chronic ulcers are case-mix diagnoses. Additional points may be earned if the* *patient is receiving IV therapy, depending on the episode and the number of therapy visits.*

A **surgical wound** results from a surgical procedure. Assign an aftercare V code, unless complicated. The disease/condition requiring the surgery will determine the appropriate surgical aftercare code. Remember, this is determined by the specific codes that are listed after *"Conditions classifiable to"* for the surgical aftercare codes.

Surgical debridement is considered a treatment and is ***not*** a surgical wound. An ulcer that is surgically debrided remains an ulcer. An incision and drainage (I&D) is also considered a treatment and does ***not*** create a surgical wound, unless there was a drain. An abscess remains an abscess, unless it is excised and there is no infection. The wound then becomes a surgical wound, and you would code the surgical aftercare. The same is true for a cyst. If there is a complication, such as an infection, code the condition (e.g., abscess, cyst). If there is no complication following an I&D, you may code surgical aftercare, but this does ***not*** make it a surgical wound for the OASIS.

Uncomplicated surgical wounds are <u>never</u> coded as a diagnosis. V58.31, Attention to surgical dressings, is only used for uncomplicated surgical wounds.

Surgical wound complications are coded as wound complications. Category 998 includes surgical complications, such as dehiscence, postoperative infection, and non-healing surgical wound, which must be supported by physician documentation.

Dehiscence takes precedence over infection, so it is coded before the infection.

Remember, do <u>**not**</u> use a V code for complicated wounds!

Note: *A non-healing surgical wound, or any other complication, cannot be based on the response to M1342 (Status of most problematic (observable) surgical wound). The diagnosis must be verified by the physician!*

Tip! *A complication code always trumps an aftercare V code, which is used for routine care only!*

If a patient had a complication of surgery and received further treatment, consider whether the condition is still complicated or if it can now be coded as aftercare. For example, if the patient had a mechanical complication of his hip prosthesis, a 996.4x code would be used to indicate the complication. If, however, the patient had a revision done and now his care is routine, code the aftercare for the joint replacement. The complication would then be coded in M1010 and M1016, if applicable.

A **trauma wound** is caused by force, violence or an accident. ***Never*** code a surgical incision or other medically caused wound as an open wound! "Open wound" means "trauma wound" in coding.

Open Wounds (870-897) are assigned only if they are due to trauma and include animal bites, avulsions, cuts, lacerations, puncture wounds and traumatic amputations. They are not associated with fracture, dislocation, internal injury, or intracranial injury.

Do not assign V58.43, aftercare following surgery for injury and trauma, unless surgery was performed and only if there are no complications.

Tip! *A sutured laceration is not considered surgery. Therefore, it is not a surgical wound. Code the laceration.*

Skin tears or partial thickness wounds are typically superficial injuries and are coded as such. If the only reason for home care is wound care to a superficial injury, Medicare does not consider this reasonable and necessary. Since the wound care is usually simple, it does not require the skills of a nurse. The skill is observation and assessment for potential complications and teaching, which can only be short-term. However, if the skin tear is complicated in some way – e.g., the tear is extensive, or no longer has a flap, or there is an underlying condition, such as diabetes or atherosclerosis, that may cause a complication, such as delayed healing – then you may code the injury as a trauma wound. For the trauma wound to be coded as primary, documentation must support that it is the focus of care, the skilled care needed, and the underlying condition, if one exists.

Burns are found in **categories 940-949**. There are detailed codes within these categories to indicate the site of the burn and to categorize the burn, such as blisters, full-thickness skin loss, or deep necrosis of underlying tissues with or without loss of a body part.

These categories include burns by an electrical heating appliance, electricity, flame, hot object, lightning, radiation, chemical burns, and scalds. They do ***not*** include sunburn or friction burns.

Code the location and severity of the burn. Code the worst burn first. Classify burns of the same local site but of different degrees to the highest degree recorded. For example, if your patient has 1st, 2nd, and 3rd degree burns on the wrist, code the 3rd degree burn only. When coding multiple burns, assign separate codes for each burn site.

Code the extent of body surface involved for any burn which includes a 3rd degree burn (Category 948). Also, code 948, if there are other burns, such as 2nd degree burns, that are extensive. Do ***not*** code 948 in home care as primary. Category 948 is used for unspecified site of the burn or to indicate the extent of the burn. It should be used as a secondary code to indicate the percentage of the body surface that is burned and the percentage of the body surface with third degree burns. The percentages of body surface are determined based on the "Rule of Nines."

A non-healing burn is classified as an acute burn. Necrosis of burned skin should also be coded as an acute burn.

If documentation supports an infected burn site, assign code 958.3, Post traumatic wound infection, not elsewhere classified, as an additional code. For example, an infected burn of the forearm is coded 943.01, 958.3.

Assign V58.43, aftercare following surgery for injury and trauma, only if surgery was performed and there are no complications.

The series of "late effects" of burns, 906.5-906.9, are for cases of healed burn sites that have a residual of the burn, such as scarring. The residual is coded first, followed by the late effect code. For example, contractures to the wrist from a burn 3 years ago are coded:

- 709.2 Cicatrix
- 906.6 Late effect of burn of wrist

Note: *Post-operative complications, traumatic wounds and burns are case-mix diagnoses in the Skin 1 group, when listed as the primary <u>or</u> secondary diagnosis. Additional points may be earned if the patient is receiving IV therapy, depending on the episode and the number of therapy visits.*

Tip! *A patient can have a non-healed burn and a late effect of another burn that has healed at the same time.*

Infections

An infection is a complication. Therefore, do ***not*** use the aftercare V codes, attention to surgical dressings, attention to artificial openings, or status codes (e.g., amputation status) related to the complication. Remember, the status code for the joint replaced, V43.6x, is always used, even when complicated. However, you may use other V codes, as applicable, such as for fitting and adjustment of vascular catheter (V58.81) and therapeutic drug monitoring (V58.83).

Code the infection first and then the causative organism, if known.

Post-surgical wound infected with Streptococcus

- 998.59, 041.00

Sometimes the infection is a combination code such as Staph aureus pneumonia. It is incorrect to code it as 486, 041.11. The correct code is one combination code which indicates that the staph caused the pneumonia – 482.41.

If resistant to antibiotics, add V09 after the organism.

- Reference the term "resistance" in the Alphabetic Index.
- More than one V09 code will be used for multiple resistance.

Tip! *V09 is not coded when a patient has a MRSA infection, unless the bacteria is also resistant to another class of antibiotics, such as Vancomycin.*

Coding Example:

Patient was admitted for administration of IV Vancomycin for 4 weeks, lab draws for peak and trough levels, and daily wound care to a dehisced surgical wound infected with MRSA.

M1020a	998.30	Disruption of wound, unspecified
M1022b	998.59	Other postoperative infection
M1022c	041.12	Methicillin-resistant Staph aureus

M1022d	V58.81	Fitting and adjustment of vascular catheter
M1022e	V58.83	Encounter for therapeutic drug monitoring
M1022f	V58.62	Long-term (current) use of antibiotics

***Note:** There is no indication in this scenario whether the dehiscence is internal (998.31) or external (998.32). This should be determined for more specificity. Dehiscence of an amputation stump is coded to 997.69. There is also a code for dehiscence of a trauma wound that was repaired by a physician (988.33). The long-term use of antibiotics is coded after therapeutic drug monitoring, since V58.83 gives the instruction to "Use an additional code for any associated long-term (current) drug use." Short-term use of antibiotics would **not** be coded.*

Complication versus Late Effect

A **complication** is a problem that arises and complicates the healing process of the initial illness, injury, or medical/surgical procedure. There is no time limit as to when a complication may occur.

Complications are generally found in categories 996-999. Look in the Alphabetic Index under the specific condition or "Complications," then verify the code in the Tabular List and follow the directions to use additional codes.

Remember, do **not** use a V code with a complication, unless instructed by the code book to do so! For example, do not use amputation status code V49.7x when there is an amputation stump complication – 997.6x.

Complication Examples:

Acute cystitis due to indwelling urinary catheter

996.64	Infection due to indwelling urinary catheter
595.0	Acute cystitis

***Note:** V53.6, Fitting and adjustment of urinary catheter is not coded, since the complication is due to the catheter. It cannot be assumed that the infection is catheter-related. This must be confirmed by the MD!*

Infection of cystostomy with cellulitis of the abdomen due to staphylococcus aureus

596.81 Infection of cystostomy

682.2 Cellulitis of abdomen

041.11 Staphylococcus aureus

Note: *V55.5, Attention to cystostomy, is **not** coded, due to the complication.*

Dislocation of prosthetic hip joint

996.42	Dislocation of prosthetic joint
V43.64	Hip joint replaced

Note this exception to the rule:

Subcategory 996.4 and subclassification 996.66 instruct to "use an additional code to identify the prosthetic joint affected."

Tip! *The status codes for the joint replaced (V43.60-V43.69) are used with any joint replacement, even when complicated.*

Not all conditions that occur during or following medical care or surgery are classified as complications. There must be a cause-and-effect relationship between the care provided and the condition, and an indication in the documentation that it is a complication. Query the physician for clarification if the complication is not clearly documented.

A **late effect** is the residual effect (condition produced) after the acute phase of an illness or injury has terminated. There is no time limit on when a late effect code can be used. The residual may be apparent early, such as an infection of the central nervous system, or it may occur months or years later, such as that due to a previous injury.

When coding a late effect, reference the word "late" in the Alphabetic Index. Coding of late effects generally requires two codes sequenced as follows:

- First – the condition or nature of the late effect (residual)
- Second – the cause of the late effect

You must know the code for the underlying injury or other cause.

- For example, gait abnormality as a late effect of hip fracture (820.8)
  - 781.2 Abnormality of gait
  - 905.3 Late effect of hip fracture (Late effect of injury classifiable to 820).

Late effects can also be found in the E Code Index immediately following the Table of Drugs and Chemicals.

There are some exceptions to this rule:

- Late effect combination codes, such as late effects of CVA, combine the presenting problem with the late effect code in one code – e.g., Late effect CVA, hemiplegia, non-dominant side, 438.22 – or two codes – e.g., Late effect CVA, dysphagia, 438.82, 787.2x.
- Some late effects are actually manifestation codes. For example, curvature of the spine as a late effect of Ricketts, is coded with the late effect first, since a manifestation code must always be preceded by its etiology – 268.1, 737.40.

The code for the acute phase of an illness or injury is <u>never</u> used with a code for the late effect. For example, never code viral encephalitis with late effects of the same condition.

More Late Effect Examples:

- Spastic hemiplegia of dominant side as a result of a traumatic brain injury (854.0x)
  - 342.11 Spastic hemiplegia affecting dominant side
  - 907.0 Late effect of intracranial injury (injury classifiable to 850-854)
- Malunion of a wrist fracture (814.00)
  - 733.81 Malunion of fracture
  - 905.2 Late effect of fracture of upper extremity (injury classifiable to 810-819)

- Weakness as a late effect of CVA *(Exception to the rule!)*
  - 438.89 Other late effects of cerebrovascular disease
  - 728.87 Muscle weakness (generalized)
- Osteopathy as a late effect of polio *(Exception to the rule!)*
  - 138 Late effects of acute poliomyelitis
  - 730.7x Osteopathy resulting from poliomyelitis

Questions for the Expert

Signs and symptoms

Q: How do you know when to code a sign or symptom vs. when it's part of a disease?

A: Some integral symptoms are obvious, such as dyspnea in COPD or edema in CHF. Sometimes they are not so obvious. If you are unsure whether a symptom is integral to the disease process, refer to medical resources to determine the symptomology of the condition you are coding.

Wound coding

Q: What wound coding information will be covered on the exam?

A: You need to know how to code ulcers, trauma wounds, and surgical wounds. If surgery was performed, you will most likely select an aftercare code, unless it is complicated. You will need to determine if the aftercare is the focus of care for appropriate sequencing. V58.31, the code for surgical dressing changes, is never coded when there is a complication and is never primary on this exam. Remember, a sutured laceration is a trauma wound and is not considered surgery.

Diagnosis codes

Q: What diagnosis codes must match across the OASIS, the CMS-485 (plan of care) and the billing claim form (UB-04)?

A: The Medicare Claims Processing Manual says that **all** of the diagnosis codes must match across all three forms – the OASIS, plan of care and billing claim.

Case-mix codes

Q: How do we know when we have a case-mix code, and how do we identify it?

A: Case-mix diagnoses are identified by a symbol in most coding manuals. So, when you look up the code in the Tabular List, you should see whether or not it is case-mix. Symbols will vary with different publishers and are noted on the bottom of the Tabular List pages. It is imperative that you know what these symbols mean! There is a case-mix diagnosis list on the CMS website (*www.cms.hhs.gov*).

The test does not ask questions on the number of points awarded or which equation a variable occurs in. However, you are expected to understand how case-mix works within the PPS system.

OASIS-C and coding

Q: Where can I find the guidance for coding the diagnosis items on the OASIS?

A: Refer to Appendix D, the OASIS guidance on selecting and sequencing diagnoses, in the OASIS-C Guidance Manual.

V and E code sequencing

Q: I've read that V codes should be sequenced at the end, unless the V code is a main focus for the encounter or is one of the three that are case-mix. Is this true for E codes as well? I know E codes are not allowed as the primary diagnosis, but should they be placed at the end?

A: Unless reporting an adverse effect or poisoning, E codes should be sequenced at the bottom of the list as well. This will leave space for more pertinent diagnoses that may be case-mix and those that are risk-adjusted.

Coding convention

Q: When the code book instructs to "use an additional code," does it matter where that code is placed?

A: Whenever coding instructions tell you to "use an additional code," it means you should sequence the additional code(s) after the one with this instruction. In coding some situations, such as etiology/manifestation combinations, late effects, pressure ulcers and organisms causing infections, the additional code should be sequenced immediately following the code that gives the instruction to use an additional code. In other instances, such as status codes – e.g., the joint replaced, the organ transplanted, or certain aftercare codes, such as attention to dressings – they may be sequenced after the numeric codes.

CVA coding exceptions

Q: What are the exceptions for coding acute CVAs?

A: There is no longer an exception to the PPS rule for home care. You must code late effects of cerebrovascular disease (Category 438) for all home health patients admitted following an acute CVA or TIA with neurologic deficits as a result of a condition classifiable to categories 430-437. If there are no neurologic deficits, code the history code for TIA and CVA – V12.54.

Late effects CVA

Q: When coding late effect CVA, what diagnosis goes in M1024?

A: Category 438 codes are case-mix diagnoses in the Neuro 3 diagnosis group. Therefore, if a V code, such as V57 for therapy only, replaces a CVA late effect, code the appropriate 438 code(s) in M1022 only, since the condition still exists. No code would be placed in M1024.

Aftercare following knee replacement

Q: If a patient is referred following a total knee replacement, what would be the aftercare code?

A: V54.81, Aftercare following joint replacement, is the specific code for joint replacement. This code is also used when the joint replacement is performed due to a trauma fracture.

Coding abnormality of gait

Q: There seems to be a lot of confusion on when to code abnormality of gait. What do we need to know on the test?

A: Whether to code abnormality of gait for lower extremity fractures and joint replacements has been one of the most discussed issues in home care coding! It is the consensus of coding experts that an abnormal gait is integral to lower extremity fractures and, therefore, it is not necessary to code it. Guidance in the Coding Clinic, 2011 Q1, instructs that coders

may code abnormality of gait, a symptom, following joint replacements. This should be decided on a case-by-case basis.

Regarding the test, 781.2, abnormality of gait, will not be a deciding factor in a scenario. However, you do need to know when to code abnormality of gait vs. difficulty in walking.

Nursing care and therapy codes

Q: Is it true that, if nursing is in on the case at all, even in lesser frequency, we should not use therapy V codes?

A: That is true. There is a coding guideline that instructs the coder to use V57 as the primary diagnosis when the encounter is for therapy only. If nursing is ordered for any number of visits, except to do the admission for therapy, V57 is not to be used. If a care plan is established for nursing, it is ***not*** a therapy-only case.

Determining the primary diagnosis on multidiscipline cases

Q: I have a patient whom nursing is monitoring 1W3 for CHF and therapy is treating 2W4 for muscle weakness as a result of CHF. In the past, we would code V57 for the weakness and then we would code the CHF. My understanding now is that we should code the CHF as primary and the muscle weakness as secondary, even though therapy is going more frequently. Is that correct?

A: It depends. Don't look at the frequencies, look at the conditions. If the patient's muscle weakness is truly the primary reason for home care, then code the muscle weakness as primary. If CHF is the most acute condition – for example, if the patient has new medications or breathing treatments, and has muscle weakness as a result of decompensating, then CHF should be coded first. If the muscle weakness is due to the exacerbated CHF, consider if it is even necessary to code it, since it would be expected that the patient would be weak. Do not code V57 as the primary diagnosis, since the case is not therapy-only.

HCS-D Certification Outline

Home Care Coding Specialist – Diagnosis (HCS-D)

This outline is designed to provide representative examples of the issues covered on the HCS-D certification examination. It is not inclusive of every issue addressed within the examination. Exam-takers must understand basic competencies, like the ones listed below.

Important Note: *The HCS-D certification exam follows the 2013 PPS Final Rule instructions for M1024, effective January 1, 2013.*

OASIS, Coding and Relationship to PPS

- Diagnosis-related forms – OASIS, POC, UB-04
- Primary (M1020) and Other (M1022) diagnoses
- Payment diagnoses (M1024)
- Case-mix and case-mix diagnosis
- Sequencing of V and E codes

Basic Coding Concepts

- Selecting principal and other (secondary) diagnoses
- Manifestation coding and conventions for identifying manifestation codes
- Coding conventions, such as essential modifiers, italics, NOS, NEC
- Appropriate use of V codes and E codes
- Sequencing, including application of coding conventions and critical thinking
- Assignment of comorbidities
- Coding symptoms
- Proximal vs. underlying conditions
- Integral conditions

Application of Coding Concepts to Home Care

- Surgical aftercare, surgical wounds and underlying conditions
- Complication codes vs. aftercare V codes vs. late effects
- Injury and trauma codes
- Combination coding and multiple coding for a single condition
- Poisoning and adverse effects
- CVAs
- Manifestations of diabetes and choosing the correct 5th digit
- Acute fracture coding – traumatic and pathologic
- Neoplasms – primary and secondary malignancies
- Medical terminology incorporated into scenarios
- Selecting the primary and other diagnoses from diagnostic statements
- Hypertensive heart disease and heart failure
- Anemia – unspecified and when due to other factors
- Dementia

Note on testing: *A case-mix diagnosis list will not be provided to test-takers. All major publishers include symbols within the code book indicating which codes are case-mix. This will be sufficient for the exam.*

HCS-D Certification Practice Questions

1. Which of the following statements is ***true***?
   a. All diagnoses treated during an inpatient stay should be coded.
   b. Numeric codes and V codes require a symptom control rating.
   c. All diagnoses must match on the OASIS, plan of care and billing claim form (UB04).
   d. There are 80 case-mix weights.

2. Which of the following statements about the primary diagnosis is ***false***?
   a. It is the chief reason for providing skilled services.
   b. It best reflects the care being provided for the entire episode.
   c. It is the condition most related to the current home health care plan.
   d. It may be a numeric code, V code or E code.

3. Which statement about other (secondary) diagnoses that should be coded is ***false***:
   a. Any diagnosis that the patient has in addition to the primary diagnosis
   b. Pertinent diagnoses relevant to the care being rendered
   c. Any comorbidity that may affect the patient's response to treatment or rehabilitation prognosis
   d. Conditions that require clinical evaluation, therapeutic treatment, extended stay, or increased monitoring

4. Which of the following comorbidities should always be coded, even if it is not actively being treated?
   a. Anemia
   b. GERD

c. Hypertension
d. Hypothyroidism

5. An italicized code in slanted brackets *[ ]* in Volume 2 indicates it is:
   a. The etiology
   b. A manifestation
   c. An unspecified code
   d. A nonessential modifier

6. Which of the following may be listed as other (secondary) diagnoses?
   a. Numeric codes
   b. V codes
   c. E codes
   d. All of the above

7. Which of the following about etiology/manifestation coding is ***false***?
   a. The etiology must be sequenced immediately before the manifestation.
   b. The manifestation may be sequenced before the etiology, if it is the focus of care.
   c. A manifestation may never be the primary diagnosis or coded without its etiology.
   d. The letter 'M' in the CMS case-mix list identifies a manifestation code.

8. Which of the following is ***not*** an example of an etiology/manifestation pairing?
   a. 250.70, 785.4
   b. 446.0, 581.81
   c. 682.2, 041.10
   d. 255.41, 359.5

9. If a V code replaces an acute fracture code in M1020 or M1022:
   a. Place it in M1024 only.
   b. Place it in M1024 and M1022.
   c. Place it in M1022 only.
   d. Do not place it in M1024 or M1022.

10. V codes are used when:
    a. There is a complication of medical or surgical care.
    b. They are more specific to the care being rendered than a medical diagnosis.
    c. A patient has a resolving disease or injury.
    d. b and c

11. Which of the following statements about E codes is ***false***?
    a. E codes identify external causes of injury or poisoning.
    b. E codes should not be used if the patient did not suffer an injury as the result of an accident or did not have an adverse effect or poisoning.
    c. E codes may never be used as a primary or payment diagnosis.
    d. E codes must always be used to indicate the cause of trauma wounds and trauma fractures.

12. Code the following:
    a. Congestive heart failure due to hypertension with pulmonary edema __________
    b. Atherosclerosis with gangrene and ulcer of ankle __________
    c. Abscess following gastric band procedure due to staphylococcus aureus __________
    d. Anemia due to chemotherapy __________
    e. Acute MI of inferolateral wall upon admission to home health __________
    f. Pressure ulcer on hip covered with eschar and slough ______

g. Therapeutic drug monitoring for anticoagulant use due to new onset of atrial fibrillation __________
h. Parkinson's dementia with wandering __________
i. Memory loss __________
j. Blisters on lower legs due to weeping edema caused by CHF __________
k. Diabetic macular edema __________
l. Stage IV gangrenous pressure ulcer on buttock and stable diabetes mellitus __________
m. Dermatitis due to Penicillin __________
n. Venous thrombosis of the cephalic vein __________
o. Papilloma of leg __________

13. What is the correct sequence for a patient admitted for PT only with an unsteady gait and recent fall due to Alzheimer's disease?
   a. 331.0, 719.7, V57.1, V15.88
   b. V15.88 (M1024 = 781.2), 781.2, 331.0
   c. V57.1, V15.88, 331.0, 719.7
   d. V57.1, 781.2, 331.0, V15.88

14. A patient with a neurogenic bladder due to multiple sclerosis is being recertified for a monthly Foley catheter change. She is on long-term antibiotics because of her history of recurrent urinary tract infections. The correct coding sequence for this scenario is:
   a. V58.62 (M1024 = 599.0), 340, 596.54, V53.6
   b. 340, 596.54, V53.6 (M1024 = 340), V13.02, V58.62
   c. V53.6, 596.54, 340, V13.02, V58.62
   d. V53.6 (M1024 = 340), 596.54, 340, 599.0, V58.62

15. A patient is admitted for treatment of infected diabetic toe ulcers on her left foot and management of her type 2 uncontrolled diabetes mellitus. Her insulin dose has required frequent readjustment. She also has PVD and poor vision due to diabetic retinopathy. The proper coding sequence for this scenario is:

    a. V58.30 (M1024 = 250.82, 707.15), 443.81, 250.52, 362.01, V58.67

    b. 250.82, 707.15, 443.9, 250.52, 362.01, V58.67

    c. 707.15, 250.82, 443.81, 250.72, 362.01, 250.52, V58.67

    d. 250.80, 707.15, 443.9, 250.50, 362.01, V58.30, V58.67

16. Your agency is administering IV antibiotics for 3 days to a patient with a laceration of the finger with cellulitis. What is the appropriate code sequence?

    a. 883.0, 682.4, V58.81

    b. 681.00, 883.0, V58.81, V58.62

    c. 883.1, 681.00, V58.81

    d. 682.4, 883.1, V58.81, V58.62

17. Which of the following is an ***incorrect*** coding of a late effect?

    a. 438.82, 787.20

    b. 907.3, 781.3

    c. 733.81, 905.3

    d. 438.21

18. The correct code assignment for a gastric bleed resulting from a cumulative effect of Coumadin being taken prophylactically due to a history of pulmonary embolism is:

    a. 964.2, 578.9, E858.2, V12.51

    b. 578.9, 964.2, V12.55

    c. 578.9, E858.2, V12.51

    d. 578.9, E934.2, V12.55

19. Your agency admitted a patient with cirrhosis of the liver who is awaiting a liver transplant. The patient is bedbound. His symptoms include jaundice, ascites, anorexia, chronic urticaria and generalized weakness. Nursing, PT and OT services have been ordered, with therapy being the primary focus. Which of the following is the correct coding sequence?

    a. 571.5, 782.4, 789.5, 783.0, 708.8, 780.79, V49.83, V49.84

    b. 571.5, V49.83, V49.84

    c. 571.5, V57.89, 782.4, 789.5, 783.0, 708.8, 780.79, V49.83, V49.84 V49.83, 571.5, V57.89, V49.84

    d. V49.83, 571.5, V49.84

20. Code the following scenario: A patient is admitted with chronic renal failure with pain and swelling at the peritoneal catheter exit site. The culture of the site reveals a staphylococcus aureus infection which is being treated at home with a 6-week course of IV antibiotics. Nursing is also performing wound care.

    a. 996.68, 041.11, 585.9, V58.81, V58.62

    b. V58.81, 585.9, 041.12, 998.59, V58.83, V58.62

    c. V58.83, 585.9, 041.11, 998.59, V58.81, V58.62

    d. 996.68, V58.31, 041.12, 585.9, V58.62

End of practice questions

Answers to HCS-D Certification Practice Questions

1. c

2. d

3. a

4. c

5. b

6. d

7. b

8. c

9. a

10. d

11. d

12. a. 402.91, 428.0 (Pulmonary edema is integral to heart failure.)

    b. 440.24, 707.13

    c. 539.01, 682.2, 041.11

    d. 285.3

    e. 410.22

    f. 707.04, 707.25

    g. 427.31, V58.83, V58.61

    h. 332.0, 294.11, V40.31

    i. 780.93

    j. 709.8 (CHF would also be coded.)

    k. 250.50, 362.07, 362.01

l. 707.05, 707.24, 785.4, 250.00 (Gangrene is linked to the pressure ulcer, so it is not a manifestation of diabetes.)

m. 693.0, E930.0

n. 453.81

o. 216.7

13. d

14. c

15. b

16. c

17. b

18. d

19. b (Symptoms integral to the liver disease would not be coded.)

20. a

HCS-D Recertification Outline

Home Care Coding Specialist – Diagnosis (HCS-D)

This outline is designed to provide representative examples of the issues covered on the HCS-D recertification examination, which addresses applicable changes for the past two years. It is not inclusive of every issue addressed within the examination.

Important Note: *The HCS-D recertification exam follows the 2013 PPS Final Rule instructions for M1024, effective January 1, 2013.*

Examination Concepts

Because this is a recertification exam, all test-takers should already know, and be up-to-date on, the coding conventions, official guidelines, and basic concepts, such as diagnosis selection and sequencing, including comorbidities, payment diagnoses and etiology/manifestation pairings. The items listed below are more specific areas you must understand.

- CVA and TIA – with and without residuals
- Dementia
- Diabetes – 4th and 5th digits
- Hypertensive heart disease and heart failure
- Neoplasms – primary and secondary malignancies
- Pain codes
- Symptom coding
  - Disease versus symptom
  - Symptoms integral to the disease process
- Complications and late effects
- V codes
  - Aftercare surgical codes
  - Status codes
  - V57 as primary only

- E codes
    - Adverse effect vs. poisoning
- Wounds
    - Ulcers
    - Surgical
    - Trauma
- Infections
    - Organisms
    - Sequencing

HCS-D Recertification Practice Questions

1. Which of the following is the correct code assignment for a patient with congestive heart failure due to acute diastolic heart failure due to hypertension?
   a. 428.0, 428.31, 401.9
   b. 402.91, 428.31, 428.0
   c. 428.0, 428.31, 402.91
   d. 401.9, 428.31, 428.0

2. You are coding the SOC assessment for a patient who was admitted for wound care to an abdominal surgical wound infected with staphylococcus following a cholecystectomy due to acute cholecystitis. Which codes would you select?
   a. 998.59, 041.10
   b. 879.3, 041.10
   c. V58.75 (M1024 = 575.0), 575.0, 041.10, V58.31
   d. 041.10, 998.59, V58.31

3. A patient is admitted for SN, PT and OT following a CVA resulting in hemiplegia of his dominant side and recurrent seizures. He has episodes of uncontrollable crying, which the doctor documented as pseudobulbar affect due to the CVA. The H&P notes a history of end-stage COPD. He is on continuous oxygen and is bedbound. Which of the following is the correct coding?
   a. V49.84, 438.21, 780.39, 310.81, 496, V46.2
   b. 434.91, 342.91, 780.39, 310.81, 491.21, V46.2, V49.84
   c. 438.21, 438.89, 345.80, 310.81, 491.21, V46.2, V49.84
   d. 438.21, 345.80, 310.81, 496, V46.2, V49.84

4. A patient is being recertified with a new onset of CHF and for a suprapubic catheter change every 60 days. She currently has an infection of her cystostomy due to gram negative bacteria and cellulitis of the skin around the ostomy. She also has dementia. How would you code this?

   a. 428.0, 997.5, 682.2, 041.85, 294.21, V55.5

   b. V55.5, 997.5, 682.2, 041.85, 428.0, 294.8

   c. 596.81, 428.0, 041.85, 682.2, 294.10, V55.5

   d. 428.0, 596.81, 682.2, 041.85, 294.20

5. A type 1 diabetic patient is admitted for aftercare following an amputation of his right foot due to diabetic PVD. His insulin dose was increased due to fluctuating blood sugars, and he has exacerbated hypertension. The H&P notes chronic kidney disease due to his diabetes and GERD, which is controlled with medication and diet. Which coding sequence is correct?

   a. V58.73, 250.71, 443.9, 401.9, 250.41, 585.9, 530.81, V49.73, V58.67

   b. V58.78 (M1024 = 250.73, 443.81), 250.73, 443.81, 250.43, 403.90, 585.9, V49.73

   c. V58.73, 250.71, 443.81, 250.41, 403.90, 585.9, V49.73

   d. V58.78, 250.73, 443.9, 401.9, 250.43, 585.9, 530.81, V49.73, V58.67

6. Select the correct codes for a patient who has lung cancer with metastasis to the lymph nodes and is referred for nursing with nausea, vomiting and dehydration from chemotherapy and management of his neoplasm-related pain. He will receive IV hydration.

   a. V58.81, 787.01, 276.51, 162.9, 196.9, 338.3

   b. 162.9, 196.9, 787.01, 276.51, E933.1, 338.3, V58.81

   c. V58.11, V58.81, 787.01, 276.51, 196.9, 162.9

   d. 162.9, 196.9, E933.1, 787.01, 276.51, 338.3, V58.81

7. An 86 year old patient is admitted for SN, PT and OT following a total hip replacement due to a traumatic fracture. He takes Boniva (a bisphosphonate) for osteoporosis. Therapy will provide the most intensive services. The correct coding sequence for this scenario is:
   a. V54.81 (M1024 = 820.8), 733.00, V43.64, V58.68
   b. V54.13 (M1024 = 820.8), 733.01, V43.64, V58.68
   c. V57.89, V54.13, 820.8, 733.00, V58.68
   d. V58.43 (M1024 = 820.8), 733.01, V58.68

8. One month later, the above patient's prosthetic hip joint became infected with MRSA. The joint was removed and replaced with an antibiotic impregnated cement spacer. He completed a course of IV antibiotics while in the hospital and was sent home on oral antibiotics. He will be scheduled for insertion of a new joint prosthesis in 6-8 weeks. How would you code the ROC assessment on this patient?
   a. V54.82 (M1024 = 996.66), 733.00, V88.21, V58.68
   b. 041.12, 996.66, 733.01, V58.68
   c. 996.66, 041.12, V09.0, 733.01, V58.68
   d. 996.66, 041.12, 733.00, V88.21, V58.68

9. Two months later, the same patient had a new hip prosthesis inserted, and he has been re-admitted to home health for PT and OT only. What are the correct codes?
   a. V54.81, 733.01, V43.64, V58.68
   b. V57.89, V54.82, 733.00, V43.64, V58.68
   c. V54.82, 733.00, V88.21, V58.68
   d. V57.89, V54.81, 733.01, V43.64, V58.68

10. Choose the correct coding sequence for a patient confined to a wheelchair due to multiple sclerosis, who is admitted for wound care to a non-healing stage III pressure ulcer on the ischial tuberosity and infected stage II pressure ulcers on the coccyx and sacrum.
    a. 340, 707.04, 707.23, 707.03, 707.22, V58.30, V46.3
    b. 707.23, 707.05, 707.22, 707.03, 340, V46.3
    c. 707.05, 707.23, 707.03, 707.22, 340, V46.3
    d. V58.30, 707.04, 707.23, 707.03, 707.22, 340, V46.3

11. How would you code a patient with diabetic polyneuropathy resulting from long-term steroid use for chronic asthmatic bronchitis?
    a. 250.60, 357.2, 493.90, V58.65
    b. 249.00, 357.2, 493.22, V58.65, E932.0
    c. V58.65, 493.90, 249.60, 357.2
    d. 249.60, 357.2, E932.0, 493.20, V58.65

12. What is the correct aftercare code following an ORIF for a traumatic ankle fracture?
    a. V54.19
    b. V54.29
    c. V58.43
    d. V54.09

13. Which of the following is the correct sequencing for spastic hemiplegia of the dominant side following an intracranial injury?
    a. 907.0, 342.11
    b. 342.11, 907.0
    c. 342.11, 854.00
    d. 854.00, 342.11

14. A patient is admitted for monitoring of his unstable benign hypertension and acute bronchitis with acute exacerbation of COPD. He is now on oxygen. He also has diastolic heart failure, dyspnea with minimal exertion, dementia with aggressive behavior and Parkinson's disease. Select the correct coding sequence.

    a. 401.1, 491.21, 491.22, 428.30, 332.0, 294.11, V46.2

    b. 401.1, 466.0, 491.21, 428.30, 294.11, 332.0, V46.2

    c. 401.1, 491.22, 428.30, 294.21, 332.0, V46.2

    d. 401.1, 491.22, 428.30, 786.09, 332.0, 294.11, V46.2

15. A patient took an accidental overdose of Lasix, which he takes for CHF. Now he is dehydrated and weak. Select the correct coding sequence.

    a. 428.0, 974.4, 276.51, 728.87, E858.5

    b. E858.5, 276.51, 780.79, 428.0

    c. 276.51, 728.87, E858.5, 428.0

    d. 974.4, 276.51, 780.79, E858.5, 428.0

End of practice questions

Answers to HCS-D Recertification Practice Questions

1. b
2. a
3. c
4. d
5. c
6. b
7. a
8. d
9. b
10. c
11. d
12. a
13. b
14. c
15. d

Note: *More practice questions can be found on the BMSC website. Go to www.medicalspecialtycoding.com and review the study materials.*

Case-Mix Adjustment Variables and Scores Table

This table, formerly Table 2A of the final PPS rule (CMS-1541-FC), shows the interaction of case-mix categories and OASIS items that can trigger case-mix points, and in which equations they trigger points. (*www.cms.gov/HomeHealthPPS/05_CaseMixGrouperSoftware.asp*).

ROW	VARIABLE DESCRIPTION	POINTS by SCORING EQUATION			
	CLINICAL DIMENSION	**1**	**2**	**3**	**4**
1	Primary or Other Diagnosis = Blindness/Low Vision	3	3	3	3
2	Primary or Other Diagnosis = Blood disorders	2	5	0	0
3	Primary or Other Diagnosis = Cancer, selected benign neoplasms	3	8	3	10
4	Primary Diagnosis = Diabetes	5	13	1	8
5	Other Diagnosis = Diabetes	3	5	1	5
6	Primary or Other Diagnosis = Dysphagia AND Primary or Other Diagnosis = Neuro 3 – Stroke	2	6	0	6
7	Primary or Other Diagnosis = Dysphagia AND M1030 (Therapy at home) = 3 (Enteral)	0	6	0	0
8	Primary or Other Diagnosis = Gastrointestinal disorders	2	6	1	5
9	Primary or Other Diagnosis = Gastrointestinal disorders AND M1630 (ostomy) = 1 or 2	2	0	0	0
10	Primary or Other Diagnosis = Gastrointestinal disorders AND Primary or Other Diagnosis = Neuro 1 – Brain disorders and paralysis, OR Neuro 2 – Peripheral neurological disorders, OR Neuro 3 – Stroke, OR Neuro 4 – Multiple Sclerosis	0	0	2	0
11	Primary or Other Diagnosis = Heart Disease OR Hypertension	3	6	1	7
12	Primary Diagnosis = Neuro 1 – Brain disorders and paralysis	3	8	5	8
13	Primary or Other Diagnosis = Neuro 1 – Brain disorders and paralysis AND M1840 (Toileting) = 2 or more	3	10	3	10
14	Primary or Other Diagnosis = Neuro 1 – Brain disorders and paralysis OR Neuro 2 – Peripheral neurological disorders AND M1810 or M1820 (Dressing upper or lower body) = 1, 2, or 3	1	4	1	2
15	Primary or Other Diagnosis = Neuro 3 – Stroke	0	2	0	0
16	Primary or Other Diagnosis = Neuro 3 – Stroke AND M1810 or M1820 (Dressing upper or lower body) = **1, 2,** or 3	1	3	2	8

ROW	VARIABLE DESCRIPTION	POINTS by SCORING EQUATION			
	CLINICAL DIMENSION	**1**	**2**	**3**	**4**
17	Primary or Other Diagnosis = Neuro 3 – Stroke AND M1860 (Ambulation) = 4 or more	1	5	0	0
18	Primary or Other Diagnosis = Neuro 4 – Multiple Sclerosis AND AT LEAST ONE OF THE FOLLOWING: M1830 (bathing) = 2 or more OR M1840 (Toileting) = 2 or more OR M1850 (Transferring) = 2 or more OR M1860 (Ambulation) = 4 or more	3	3	12	18
19	Primary or Other Diagnosis = Ortho 1 – Leg Disorders or Gait Disorders AND M1324 (most problematic pressure ulcer stage) = 1, 2, 3 or 4	2	0	0	0
20	Primary or Other Diagnosis = Ortho 1 – Leg OR Ortho 2 – Other orthopedic disorders AND M1030 (Therapy at home) = 1 (IV/Infusion) or 2 (Parenteral)	5	5	0	0
21	Primary or Other Diagnosis = Psych 1 – Affective and other psychoses, depression	4	6	2	6
22	Primary or Other Diagnosis = Psych 2 – Degenerative and other organic psychiatric disorders	1	3	0	3
23	Primary or Other Diagnosis = Pulmonary disorders	1	5	1	5
24	Primary or Other Diagnosis = Pulmonary disorders AND M1860 (Ambulation) = 1 or more	1	0	0	0
25	Primary Diagnosis = Skin 1 – Traumatic wounds, burns, and post-operative complications	10	20	8	20
26	Other Diagnosis = Skin 1 – Traumatic wounds, burns, post-operative complications	6	6	4	4
27	Primary or Other Diagnosis = Skin 1 – Traumatic wounds, burns, and post-operative complications OR Skin 2 – Ulcers and other skin conditions AND M1030 (Therapy at home) = 1 (IV/Infusion) or 2 (Parenteral)	2	0	2	0
28	Primary or Other Diagnosis = Skin 2 – Ulcers and other skin conditions	6	12	5	12
29	Primary or Other Diagnosis = Tracheostomy	4	4	4	0
30	Primary or Other Diagnosis = Urostomy/Cystostomy	6	22	4	22
31	M1030 (Therapy at home) = 1 (IV/Infusion) or 2 (Parenteral)	8	15	5	11
32	M1030 (Therapy at home) = 3 (Enteral)	4	11	0	11
33	M1200 (Vision) = 1 or more	1	0	0	2
34	M1242 (Pain) = 3 or 4	1	0	0	0
35	M1308 (Number Pressure Ulcers) = Two or more pressure ulcers at stage 3 or 4	3	3	5	5
36	M1324 (Most problematic pressure ulcer stage) = 1 or 2	5	11	5	11

ROW	VARIABLE DESCRIPTION	POINTS by SCORING EQUATION			
	CLINICAL DIMENSION	**1**	**2**	**3**	**4**
37	M1324 (Most problematic pressure ulcer stage) = 3 or 4	16	26	12	22
38	M1334 (Stasis ulcer status) = 2	7	7	7	7
39	M1334 (Stasis ulcer status) = 3	11	11	11	11
40	M1342 (Surgical wound status) = 2	0	2	3	0
41	M1342 (Surgical wound status) = 3	4	4	4	4
42	M1400 (Dyspnea) = 2, 3, or 4	2	2	0	0
43	M1620 (Bowel Incontinence) = 2 to 5	1	2	1	0
44	M1630 (Ostomy) = 1 or 2	5	9	3	9
45	M2030 (Injectable Drug Use) = 0, 1, 2 **or 3**	0	1	2	3

FUNCTIONAL DIMENSION					
46	M1810 or M1820 (Dressing upper or lower body) = 1, 2, or 3	2	4	2	2
47	M1830 (Bathing) = 2 or more	3	3	6	6
48	M1840 (Toileting) = 2 or more	2	3	2	0
49	M1850 (Transferring) = 2 or more	0	1	0	0
50	M1860 (Ambulation) = 1, 2 **or 3**	1	0	1	0
51	M1860 (Ambulation) = **4** or more	3	3	4	5

NOTE: Points are additive. However, points will ***not*** be given for the same line item in the table more than once.

Source: CMS

HH PPS Grouper, Fracture Conditions and Appropriate V Codes, 2013

When fracture aftercare V codes are reported as primary ***or*** secondary diagnoses, and paired with an eligible (numerical) fracture code in M1024, the grouper will award appropriate clinical points. Below is a list of valid fracture conditions when paired with appropriate V codes will generate case-mix points in M1024.

V code	Description	ICD pair	Description
V54.10	Aftercare for healing traumatic fracture of arm, unspecified	818.0–818.1	**Category 818** Ill-defined fracture of upper limb
V54.11	Aftercare for healing traumatic fracture of upper arm	812.00–812.03, 812.09–812.13, 812.19, 812.20–812.21, 812.30–812.31, 812.40–812.44, 812.49, 812.50–812.54, 812.59	**Category 812** Fracture of the humerus
V54.12	Aftercare for healing traumatic fracture of lower arm	813.00–813.08, 813.10–813.18, 813.20–813.23, 813.30–813.33, 813.40–813.47, 813.50–813.54, 813.80–813.83, 813.90–813.93	**Category 813** Fracture of the radius and ulna
V54.13	Aftercare for healing traumatic fracture of hip	820.00–820.03, 820.09, 820.10–820.13, 820.19, 820.20–820.22, 820.30–820.32, 820.8, 820.9	**Category 820** Fracture of neck of femur (i.e., hip fracture)
V54.14	Aftercare for healing traumatic fracture of leg, unspecified	827.0, 827.1	**Category 827** Other, multiple, and ill-defined fractures of lower limb
V54.15	Aftercare for healing traumatic fracture of upper leg	821.00–821.01, 821.10 -821.11, 821.20–821.23, 821.29, 821.30–821.33, 821.39	**Category 821** Fracture of other and unspecified parts of femur
V54.16	Aftercare for healing traumatic fracture of lower leg	822.0–822.1, 823.00–823.02, 823.10–823.12, 823.20–823.22, 823.30–823.32, 823.40–823.42, 823.80–823.82, 823.90–823.92	**Category 822** Fracture of patella **Category 823** Fracture of tibia and fibula
V54.17	Aftercare for healing traumatic fracture of vertebrae	805.00–805.08, 805.10–805.18, 805.2, 805.3, 805.4, 805.5, 805.6, 805.7, 805.8, 805.9, 806.00–806.09, 806.10–806.19, 806.20–806.29, 806.30–806.39, 806.4, 806.5, 806.60–806.62, 806.69, 806.70–806.72, 806.79, 806.8, 806.9	**Category 805** Fracture of vertebral column without mention of spinal cord injury **Category 806** Fracture of vertebral column with spinal cord injury

V code	Description	ICD pair	Description
V54.19	Aftercare for healing traumatic fracture of bone NEC	Categories 800, 801, 802, 803, 804, 807, 808, 809, 810, 811, 814, 815, 816, 817, 819, 824, 825, 828	**Category 800** Fracture of vault of skull **Category 801** Fracture of base of skull **Category 802** Fracture of face bones **Category 803** Other & unqualified skull fractures **Category 804** Multiple fractures involving skull or face with other bones **Category 807** Fracture of rib(s), sternum, larynx, and trachea **Category 808** Fracture of pelvis **Category 809** Ill-defined fractures of bones of trunk **Category 810** Fracture of clavicle **Category 811** Fracture of scapula **Category 814** Fracture of carpal bones **Category 815** Fracture of metacarpal bones **Category 816** Fracture of one or more phalanges of hand **Category 817** Multiple fractures of hand bones **Category 819** Multiple fractures involving both upper limbs, and upper limb with rib(s) and sternum **Category 824** Fracture of ankle **Category 825** Fracture of one or more tarsal and metatarsal bones **Category 828** Multiple fractures involving both lower limbs, lower with upper limb(s) and lower limb(s) with rib(s) and sternum
V54.20	Aftercare path fracture of arm NOS	733.19	Pathologic fracture of other specified site
V54.21	Aftercare path fracture of upper arm	733.11	Pathologic fracture of humerus

V code	Description	ICD pair	Description
V54.22	Aftercare path fracture of lower arm	733.12	Pathologic fracture of distal radius and ulna
V54.23	Aftercare path fracture of hip	733.14	Pathologic fracture of neck of femur
V54.24	Aftercare path fracture of leg NOS	733.19	Pathologic fracture of other specified site
V54.25	Aftercare path fracture of upper leg	733.15	Pathologic fracture of other specified part of femur
V54.26	Aftercare path fracture of lower leg	733.16	Pathologic fracture of tibia and fibula
V54.27	Aftercare path fracture of vertebrae	733.13	Pathologic fracture of vertebrae
V54.29	Aftercare path fracture of bone NEC	733.10 733.19	**733.10** Pathologic fracture unspecified site **733.19** Pathologic fracture other specified site

Source: CMS, HHS. Final Rule: Medicare Home Health Prospective Payment System Rate Update for Calendar Year 2013. (42 CFR Parts 409, 424, 484, 488, 489, and 498). Published 11/05/12.

V codes that generate primary case-mix points for diagnoses in M1022b

Effective Jan. 1, 2013, the home health Grouper will permit more codes to act "as if" they are primary when ***immediately preceded*** by a designated V code in M1020. Below is the designated list of V codes that will promote diagnoses codes placed in M1022b to score primary case-mix points. This is especially important for case-mix codes in the diabetes, skin 1 and neuro 1 categories as they garner more points when listed as primary versus secondary. CMS made this change to the Grouper logic as a result of the restriction placed on the use of the M1024 payment slot to only allow fracture codes.

Important: A point of confusion among coding experts is that one-third of the designated V codes below are secondary-only V codes and are not eligible to be listed in M1020 primary slot. See the designations to the right of each code (P – Primary only, S – Secondary only, or P/S – Primary/Secondary) to learn in which position the V code is permitted per coding guidelines.

P/S	V07.39	Other prophylactic chemotherapy
S	V07.51	Prophylactic use SERMs
S	V07.52	Prophylactic use aromatase inhibitors
S	V07.59	Prophylactic use of other agents affecting estrogen receptors and estrogen levels
P/S	V07.8	Prophylactic measure NEC
P/S	V07.9	Prophylactic measure NOS

S	V09.0	Infection with microorganisms resistant to penicillins
S	V09.1	Infection with microorganisms resistant to cephalosporins and other B-lactam antibiotics
S	V09.2	Infection with microorganisms resistant to macrolides
S	V09.3	Infection with microorganisms resistant to tetracyclines
S	V09.4	Infection with microorganisms resistant to aminoglycosides
S	V09.50	Infection with microorganisms resistant to multiple quinolones and fluoroquinolones without mention of resistance to multiple quinolones and fluoroquinolones
S	V09.51	With resistance to multiple quinolones and fluoroquinolones
S	V09.6	Infection with microorganisms resistant to sulfonamides
S	V09.70	Infection with microorganisms resistant to other specified antimycobacterial agents without mention of resistance to multiple antimycobacterial agents
S	V09.71	With resistance to multiple antimycobacterial agents

S	V09.80	Infection with microorganisms resistant to other specified drugs without mention of resistance to multiple drugs
S	V09.81	With resistance to multiple drugs
S	V09.90	Infection with drug-resistant microorganisms, unspecified without mention of multiple drug resistance
S	V09.91	With multiple drug resistance

S	V46.0	Dependence on aspirator
S	V46.11	Respirator dependence status
P	V46.12	Respirator dependence during power failure
P	V46.13	Weaning from respirator
P/S	V46.14	Mechanical complication of respirator
S	V46.2	Dependence on supplement oxygen
S	V46.3	Wheelchair dependence
S	V46.8	Machine dependence NEC
P/S	V46.9	Machine dependence NOS

P/S	V51.8	Aftercare plastic surgery NEC

P/S	V52.0	Fitting artificial arm
P/S	V52.1	Fitting artificial leg
P/S	V52.8	Fitting prosthesis NEC
P/S	V52.9	Fitting prosthesis NOS

P/S	V53.6	Fitting urinary devices
P/S	V53.7	Fitting orthopedic devices
P/S	V53.8	Adjustment of wheelchair
P/S	V53.90	Fitting/adjustment device NOS
P/S	V53.91	Fitting/adjustment insulin pump
P/S	V53.99	Fitting/adjustment device NEC

P/S	V54.09	Aftercare internal fixation device
P/S	V54.81	Aftercare joint replacement
P/S	V54.82	Aftercare following explantation of joint prosthesis
P/S	V54.89	Orthopedic aftercare NEC
P/S	V54.9	Orthopedic aftercare NOS

P/S	V55.1	Attention to gastrostomy
P/S	V55.2	Attention to ileostomy
P/S	V55.3	Attention to colostomy
P/S	V55.4	Attention to enterostomy NEC
P/S	V55.7	Attention artificial vagina
P/S	V55.8	Attention to artificial open NEC
P/S	V55.9	Attention to artificial open NOS

P	V57.0	Breathing exercises
P	V57.1	Physical therapy NEC
P	V57.21	Encounter for occupational therapy
P	V57.3	Speech-language therapy
P	V57.81	Orthotic training
P	V57.89	Rehabilitation procedure NEC
P	V57.9	Rehabilitation procedure NOS

P	V58.11	Antineoplastic chemotherapy encounter
P	V58.12	Antineoplastic immunotherapy encounter
P/S	V58.2	Blood transfusion, without reported diagnosis
P/S	V58.30	Attention change or removal of nonsurgical wound dressing
P/S	V58.31	Attention change or removal of surgical wound dressing
P/S	V58.32	Attention change or removal of sutures
P/S	V58.42	Aftercare neoplasm surgery
P/S	V58.43	Aftercare injury/trauma surgery
P/S	V58.44	Aftercare organ transplant
P/S	V58.49	Postoperative other specified aftercare

S	V58.61	Long-term (current) use of anticoagulants
S	V58.62	Long-term (current) use of use of antibiotics
S	V58.63	Long-term (current) use of use of antiplatelets/antithrombotics
S	V58.64	Long-term (current) use of use of anti-inflammatories
S	V58.65	Long-term (current) use of steroids
S	V58.66	Long-term (current) use of aspirin
S	V58.67	Long-term (current) use of insulin

S	V58.68	Long term (current) use of bisphosphonates
S	V58.69	Long-term (current) use of meds NEC

P/S	V58.71	Aftercare surgery sense organs NEC
P/S	V58.72	Aftercare surgery nervous system NEC
P/S	V58.73	Aftercare surgery circulatory system NEC
P/S	V58.74	Aftercare surgery respiratory system NEC
P/S	V58.75	Aftercare surgery oral cavity and digestive system NEC
P/S	V58.76	Aftercare surgery genitourinary system NEC
P/S	V58.77	Aftercare surgery skin and subcutaneous system NEC
P/S	V58.78	Aftercare surgery musculoskeletal system NEC

P/S	V58.81	Fitting and adjustment vascular catheter
P/S	V58.82	Fitting and adjustment non-vascular catheter NEC
P/S	V58.83	Therapeutic drug monitoring
P/S	V58.89	Other specified aftercare
P/S	V58.9	Aftercare NOS

Source: CMS Home Health Grouper, released Nov. 28, 2012

Advice and Facts for Test Day

- Test takers should have a current ICD-9-CM code book. No other references will be permitted.
- The certification exam contains 50 questions and allows up to 2.5 hours for test-takers. The recertification exam is 10 questions and allows up to 1.5 hours.
- Both tests are multiple choice.
- A passing grade is 78 percent or above. Since the test may be retaken if a passing grade is not achieved, there are a few versions of it.
- The test contains no trick questions. It tests knowledge of the coding guidelines and conventions and the ability to apply them. It is written by home care coding specialists with input from previous test takers.
- Remember to use both the Alphabetic Index and Tabular List to code correctly.
- Following instructional notes is key to coding accuracy.
- Ask, "What is the primary focus of care?" when beginning to code scenarios.
- Pay close attention to 4th and 5th digits and appropriate placement of case-mix diagnoses in M1024.
- Only acute fractures are placed in the payment slot on the exams.
- Be cautious when a question or answer contains qualifiers such as "always," "all," "never," and "must." If any part of the statement is not true, then the whole statement is not true.

About the Author and the BMSC Home Care Advisory Board Members

Sharon Molinari, RN, HCS-D, HCS-O, is a registered nurse and home health consultant in Las Vegas. A home health professional since 1989, she is a Board of Medical Specialty Coding & Compliance (BMSC) advisory board member and one of the test developers for the HCS-D examinations. She is also a contributor to various home health publications and authors continuing education programs for health care providers.

The Board of Medical Specialty Coding & Compliance's Home Health Advisory Board members are:

Judy Adams, RN, BSN, HCS-D, COS-C, HCS-O
President
Adams Home Care Consulting, Inc.
Chapel Hill, NC

Vonnie Blevins, RN, HCS-D, HCS-O, COS-C
Coder
Excellence in Homecare
Conetoe, NC

Arlynn Hansell, PT, HCS-D, COS-C, HCS-O
Program Manager, Clinical Excellence
American Mercy Home Care
Cincinatti, OH

Lisa Selman-Holman, JD, BSN, RN, CHCE, HCS-D, HCS-O, COS-C
President
Selman-Holman & Associates, LLC
Denton, TX

Sharon Molinari, RN, HCS-D, HCS-O
Home Health Consultant
Henderson, NV

Ann Rambusch, MSN, HCS-D, RN, COS-C, HCS-O
President
Rambusch3 Consulting
Georgetown, TX

Additional Study Resources

ICD-9-CM Coding Guidelines

www.cdc.gov/nchs/data/icd9/9cmguidelines2011.pdf

Medicare Home Health Prospective Payment System

www.cms.hhs.gov/HomeHealthPPS

Medicare Home Health Benefit Policy Manual

www.cms.hhs.gov/manuals/Downloads/bp102c07.pdf

OASIS-C Guidance Manual

www.cms.hhs.gov/HomeHealthQualityInits/14_HHQIOASISUserManual.asp

Wound Ostomy and Continence Nurses Society

www.wocn.org

Board of Medical Specialty Coding & Compliance

www.medicalspecialtycoding.com

Ethical and Legal Standards

Due to the complex regulatory requirements regarding the coding process, coding professionals are often faced with ethical challenges.

Coders are responsible for maintaining and promoting ethical standards and practices within their profession and in their interactions with other healthcare professionals.

BMSC-certified coders are expected to uphold these standards. Actions that violate the standards of the Ethics Code may lead to revocation of the certification.

Please review these standards in the *Candidate Handbook*, which is available online at *www.medicalspecialtycoding.com*.

To ensure that coders who earn the highly-esteemed HCS-D credential are knowledgeable about ethical and legal standards, the HCS-D certification examination includes related questions.

In your role as a professional coder, it's imperative that you adhere to the following rules:

- All diagnoses must be stated or confirmed by the physician.
- It is the responsibility of the assessing clinician to determine the diagnoses, in conjunction with the physician, to sequence them, and to assign the symptom control rating.
- Any changes to the OASIS assessment, including the diagnoses, must be approved by the assessing clinician.
- The diagnoses must be supported by the documentation in the medical record.
- Read all supporting documentation, including the assessing clinician's narrative note and interventions, to assure accuracy of the diagnoses coded.
- Collaborate with the assessing clinician and/or the physician to clarify conflicting diagnoses or any uncertainty.
- Comply with the official coding guidelines and OASIS guidance for the diagnosis items.

- Do not list diagnoses based solely on their case mix status.
- All diagnoses must match on the OASIS, Plan of Care, and billing claim.

Consider these situations:

1. The physician documents Alzheimer's dementia, and the nurse lists dementia then Alzheimer's, since she feels the dementia has more of an impact on the care plan. As the coder, you should:

   a. List the diagnoses as the nurse did because, since it's the assessing clinician's responsibility to determine the sequencing.

   b. Sequence Alzheimer's disease followed by dementia. It's not necessary to contact the assessing clinician, since this is a coding guideline.

   c. Follow the coding guidelines for etiology/manifestation pairings, and contact the assessing clinician for approval to make the change.

2. There's a discrepancy in physician documentation regarding the type of ulcer on the patient's lower leg. The primary care physician states it's a diabetic ulcer and the consulting vascular surgeon states it's a stasis ulcer. The assessing nurse lists diabetic ulcer as a diagnosis and completes the data items for stasis ulcer on the OASIS. What should you do?

   a. Code the ulcer as both diabetic and stasis.

   b. Do not code this until you get clarification from the assessing nurse or the physician as to the type of ulcer.

   c. Code diabetic ulcer, since this is what the primary care physician documented and the assessing clinician listed.

3. A patient was referred to your agency for SN and PT due to increased dyspnea and weakness. The physician's office nurse filled out the F2F with these diagnoses, the physician signed and dated it, and it was faxed to the agency. There's no other physician documentation. The nurse who did the SOC assessment noted the patient was started on a new bronchodilator and documented exacerbation of COPD as the primary diagnosis. Which of the following should you do?

   a. Consult with the SOC nurse to see if exacerbation of COPD was confirmed by the physician.

   b. Code dyspnea and weakness, since they're listed on the F2F.

   c. Code exacerbation of COPD, as documented by the nurse, because this is noted as the focus of care in the summary on the OASIS, and the patient is on a new bronchodilator.

4. Your agency received a referral on a patient who was admitted to the hospital with a fever, persistent cough, dyspnea with minimal exertion, and extreme weakness. She was diagnosed with pneumonia and received IV antibiotics, which were changed to oral when she was discharged to a rehab facility. Therapy services were provided for strengthening due to muscle weakness for 3 weeks. The oral antibiotics for pneumonia were discontinued 10 days prior to discharge. Which of the following statements is ***true*** regarding placement of diagnoses in M1010 (Inpatient Diagnoses) and M1016 (Diagnoses Requiring Medical or Treatment Regimen Change during the past 14 days) for this patient?

   a. All diagnoses, including documented symptoms, which were treated during the hospital stay, will be listed in M1010.

   b. Pneumonia and muscle weakness will be listed in M1010 <u>and</u> M1016, since these were treated during the rehab stay.

   c. Pneumonia will be listed in M1010 but <u>not</u> in M1016, since the antibiotics were discontinued due to an improvement in this condition.

5. The physician documented depression with anxiety on a patient admitted for exacerbation of CHF and uncontrolled hypertension. The admitting nurse lists the diagnoses as CHF – 428.0, HTN – 401.9, Depression – 311, Anxiety – 300.00, and there will be interventions on the POC for these diagnoses. You know that the code for depression with anxiety is 300.4, which is a discrepancy with what the nurse coded. What should you do?

   a. Code depression and anxiety, just as the admitting nurse did, since 311 is a case mix diagnosis.

   b. Code 300.4, since this is what the MD documented, and contact the admitting nurse for approval.

   c. Do not code either, since the depression screening did not indicate a current problem.

6. The physician doesn't approve of 2 of the diagnoses listed on the POC. He crossed them out and refused to sign it. The RAP has already been submitted. What needs to be done?

   a. Re-print the POC with the same diagnoses, since the assessing clinician says the patient definitely has these, and ask the Medical Director to sign it.

   b. Make the appropriate corrections to the POC and re-send it to the certifying physician for signature. Since neither of these diagnoses are case mix, it's not necessary to do anything regarding billing.

   c. Since the diagnoses must match on the OASIS, POC, and billing claim, the RAP will need to be cancelled and re-submitted with the appropriate codes. The POC must be corrected and re-sent to the certifying physician for signature.

Answers:

1. c
2. b
3. a
4. c
5. b
6. c